TEACHING CHILDREN MOVEMENT CONCEPTS AND SKILLS

Becoming a Master Teacher

CRAIG A. BUSCHNER, EdD
California State University, Chico

Human Kinetics

Library of Congress Cataloging-in-Publication Data

Buschner, Craig A., 1951-
    Teaching children movement concepts and skills : becoming a master
teacher / Craig A. Buschner.
        p.   cm.
    ISBN 0-87322-480-9
    1. Movement education.   I. Title.
GV452.B87   1994
372.86--dc20   93-33577
                                                               CIP

ISBN: 0-87322-480-9

Acquisitions Editor: Scott Wikgren
Series Editor: George Graham, PhD
AMTP Content Editor: Christine Hopple
Developmental Editor: Julia Anderson
Assistant Editors: Lisa Sotirelis and Dawn Roselund
Copyeditor: Anne Mischakoff Heiles
Proofreader: Holly Gilly
Production Director: Ernie Noa
Typesetting and Text Layout: Sandra Meier
Illustration Coordinators: Tara Welsch and Kris Slamans
Text Designer: Keith Blomberg
Cover Designer: Jody Boles
Photographer (cover): Bob Veltri
Cover Models: Andrew Baffi, Nick Baffi, Emily Carstenson, and Jennifer Shephard
Illustrators: Mary Yemma Long, Kathy Boudreau-Fuoss, and Gretchen Walters
Printer: United Graphics

Printed in the United States of America

10   9   8   7   6   5   4   3   2   1

Human Kinetics
Box 5076, Champaign, IL 61825-5076
1-800-747-4457

Canada: Human Kinetics, Box 24040, Windsor, ON N8Y 4Y9
1-800-465-7301 (in Canada only)

Europe: Human Kinetics, P.O. Box IW14, Leeds LS16 6TR, England
0532-781708

Australia: Human Kinetics, P.O. Box 80, Kingswood 5062, South Australia
618-374-0433

New Zealand: Human Kinetics, P.O. Box 105-231, Auckland 1
(09) 309-2259

To my parents, Mary Jane and Jim Koch, and my children, Traci and Bryan,
for your encouragement as I pursued my love for teaching, learning, children, and movement.
You have taught me more than I can ever return.

Contents

Series Preface

In the United States most children spend 6 to 7 years in elementary schools, from kindergarten through sixth grade. Assume that they participate in instructional physical education classes twice a week for the entire time. Each class is 30 minutes long—a total of 36 hours a year and 216 hours over 6 years. Because of interruptions such as snow days, field trips, school plays, absences, and arriving late to physical education class, the time actually spent in physical education may be closer to 150 hours—perhaps less. Still 150 hours is a substantial amount of time. But what do children learn in that time? What is realistic to expect they might learn?

The answers vary. Some children might learn that physical activity is enjoyable, something they choose to do on their own with friends after school and on weekends. Others might learn that they are not good at sports and search for other ways to spend their leisure time. Others might really like their PE classes and the teacher but, given a choice, prefer to watch television or sit around when they're at home. The 150 hours, hopefully more, that a child spends in physical education classes influence his or her decisions— as a child, and for a lifetime!

What do we expect children to learn in elementary school physical education? Until recently the answer to this question was left solely to the individual teacher or school district. Physical educators across the United States had no universal sense of the outcomes that might accrue from quality programs of physical education. But this changed in 1992, when the National Association for Sport and Physical Education (NASPE) completed 7 years of work on a document titled *The Physically Educated Person*. This document outlined, for the first time, a nationally developed and endorsed framework for planning and evaluating physical education programs, from preschool through Grade 12. This book, and the other volumes in this series, were developed using the outcomes and benchmarks developed by NASPE as a general guide.

As you might imagine, the American Master Teacher Program (AMTP) struggled with how to organize the content. Should there be one book? Several books? Which model should we use to organize the content? Ultimately we chose to develop five books on the following topics: basic movement concepts and skills, games, gymnastics, dance, and fitness concepts. We decided to publish several books instead of just one because it seemed to be the most widely understood approach to organizing the content in physical education. It also provided the opportunity to involve several authors who were recognized for their expertise in their respective areas.

As we were considering possible authors, we made lists of who we thought were the best qualified individuals to write these books. In each instance, we are delighted to say, the author or authors we thought most qualified accepted our invitation to write the book. The books are as follows:

- *Teaching Children Movement Concepts and Skills: Becoming a Master Teacher* by Craig Buschner
- *Teaching Children Dance: Becoming a Master Teacher* by Theresa Purcell
- *Teaching Children Gymnastics: Becoming a Master Teacher* by Peter Werner
- *Teaching Children Games: Becoming a Master Teacher* by David Belka
- *Teaching Children Fitness: Becoming a Master Teacher* by Tom and Laraine Ratliffe

In addition, we want to thank Dr. Paula Ely, principal of Margaret Beeks Elementary School in Blacksburg, VA, for her ongoing support of various aspects of the American Master Teacher Program.

Each book is divided into two parts. The first part contains five chapters, which include a description of the content, an explanation of how it is organized, and most importantly the reasons why the author or authors believe that content is important for children to learn. One problem that has plagued physical education in elementary schools is that programs all too often have lacked an underlying theory or purpose. It seemed that teachers were just trying to entertain the children rather than to actually teach them. For this reason, we hope you will begin reading this book by carefully reading Part I so that you can better understand the content—and *why* it is important for children to learn.

Part II contains the activities, or learning experiences (LEs). Four chapters contain the actual "stuff" to do with children. It is more than just stuff, however. Part II presents a logical progression of activities designed to lead children toward a heightened understanding and improved competence in the content described in the book. After you read the content described in Part I, you will be better able to envision where the LEs are leading—and the importance of the progression and sequencing of these activities will be clear to you. From the standpoint of the author, and ultimately the children, it would be unfortunate if a teacher completely skipped Part I and then searched Part II for activities that appeared to be the most fun and exciting—and then taught them in a haphazard way without any logical sequencing or order to the program. Children truly enjoy learning! These books are designed to help them do just that; the purpose is not just to keep them busy for a few minutes several times a week.

Finally, it is important to emphasize that *the contents of all five books are important* for the children's physical education. One danger in doing a series of books is that a mistaken impression might be given that a content area can be skipped altogether. This is not the case. Just as it wouldn't make sense for math teachers to skip subtraction or division because they didn't like to "take things away" or "weren't very good at it," it doesn't make sense to skip dance or gymnastics, for example, because a teacher has never had a course in it or isn't confident about teaching it. We realize, however, that many physical education teachers feel less confident about teaching dance or gymnastics; this is the primary reason the books were written—and why the AMTP was founded. It is certainly OK to feel anxious or unconfident about teaching one, or more, of the content areas. It's not OK, however, not to teach them because of these feelings. Many of us have experienced these same feelings, but with experience, work, and support, we have gradually incorporated them into our programs—and done so in ways that are both beneficial and enjoyable for children. This is what we want to help you to do as well. And that's why the books were written and the AMTP was developed.

Each of the five content books also has a companion videotape that provides examples of actual lessons selected from the learning experiences. These consolidated lessons show you how a few LEs might be developed with children. In addition to the videotapes, workshops are available through the American Master Teacher Program to help you gain a better understanding of the content and how it is taught. The authors of the books realize that making the transition from a traditional program to teaching this content is not easy, and yet increasingly teachers are realizing that children deserve more than simply being entertained in the name of physical education. We hope you will find the books worthwhile—and helpful—and that the children you teach will benefit!

George Graham
Cofounder and Director of Curriculum
    and Instruction
American Master Teacher Program

Preface

My passion for movement and interest in helping others was cultivated, as a child, on many playgrounds, ball fields, and gymnasiums in northern Virginia. I spent endless hours, much to my parents' surprise, not only practicing motor skills but studying (reading, observing, experimenting) ways to move and perform better. I found it exciting to share this knowledge with friends. For me, the process of learning was just as exciting as competing with others to win a contest. Learning how to run, throw, catch, strike, and kick were as important to me as learning to read, write, and manipulate numbers. I decided nearly two decades ago to study children formally and teach elementary physical education. Being a physical education teacher and teaching other physical educators would give me the opportunity to teach what I loved, to help children discover the rapture of movement, and to reform the field.

My professional journey, however, has been like riding the erratic rise and fall of the stock market. Movement, play, and exercise are integral to the lives of children and adults; nevertheless, forces inside and outside the profession seem to diminish the importance and support of these activities. Just as physical education appears to be on the brink of dramatic change, it loses momentum and reverts to tired thinking and old standards. This exciting profession changes with frustrating slowness. I cringe seeing school activities that still emphasize complex sport skills, relays with long lines of students, games for which children lack the prerequisite skills and knowledge, supervised recreation, and sports played to feed coaches and interscholastic teams. These programs are outmoded.

The most important aspect of elementary physical education is teaching children and youths how to perform skillful movements. Children should develop competence and confidence as they learn basic motor skills. They should not prematurely attempt complex sport skills and dances designed for adolescents and adults. Children need time to grow; they should have well-designed, relevant learning progressions.

Parting with tradition, educators are redirecting elementary physical education programs to be developmentally appropriate. They are designing programs to meet the needs of individual children based on their stage of growth and development. This approach builds a foundation of movement experiences for healthy and active lifestyles. It no longer makes sense to equate physical education for children with disparate games and relays, calisthenics, or watered-down adult sports and fitness activities. Each teacher should have a sound theoretical basis for teaching; each child should graduate from elementary school physically fit, knowing the benefits of active participation, valuing a lifetime of healthy play, and, most importantly, possessing fundamental motor skill literacy.

The purpose of this book is to encourage physical education teachers in transcending traditional beliefs and designing developmentally appropriate physical education programs for children. The metaphorical movement alphabet consisting of *movement concepts* (body awareness, space awareness, effort qualities, and relationships) and *motor skills* (locomotor and manipulative skills), is the focus of this book and lays the foundation for the four content areas (games, dance, physical fitness, gymnastics) of the companion books of the American Master Teacher Program. Together, these books comprise a curriculum model for developmentally appropriate physical education for children.

This volume is divided into two parts. Part I features five chapters that explain the rationale, context, curriculum, methods, and assessment techniques for teaching and learning the movement concepts and motor skills. It attempts to answer the three fundamental questions for any school subject: Where are you going? How will you get there? How do you know when you have arrived? Part II contains four chapters of learning experiences to stimulate teachers to transfer theory into practice, developing body and space awareness, effort and relationships, and locomotor and manipulative skills. Each LE provides the teacher with developmentally appropriate images of teaching the movement alphabet. References and suggested readings close the book.

The literature for physical education teachers discloses very few sources that are developmen-tally appropriate to children and youth. Books about having fun often have superseded meaningful teaching and learning. As in many fields, traditional practices endure, not always in the children's best interests. It is easy for educators to embrace an encyclopedic beanbag curriculum, overlooking the true contribution of physical education to the developing child. I hope this book will help readers question what and how to teach children in school physical education. It is time for educators to debunk and let go of the "20 games" approach to children's physical education.

Acknowledgments

I would like to thank those who have helped me with this book. First and foremost, George Graham has been a wonderful role model whose leadership in the field even now catalyzes my energy to see physical education change for all children. He helped publish my first article, now my first book: My involvement in the American Master Teacher Program is largely due to "the Chief."

I wish to express appreciation to Don Hellison and Wendy Mustain for their thoughtful comments on manuscript drafts. Don has become a wonderful friend and critic of my work. Wendy, a former colleague at California State University (CSU), Chico has kept my writing practical and away from paradigms.

My daughter, Traci Buschner, provided excellent substantive feedback on chapters 1 and 3 of the manuscript. It's wonderful to have an off-spring who holds a degree in English. Likewise, my son Bryan has been very patient, understanding as few 10-year-olds do, that this project was important to me. Thanks, Bry.

I am ever grateful to my students, colleagues, and friends at CSU, Chico. Graduate students Gary Towne and Vanessa Bryan worked with my manuscript for over 8 months. Gary conducted library research, typed, and edited portions of the manuscript. Vanessa, an elementary specialist in Durham, California, deserves credit for the ideas behind many illustrations. She contributed five LEs, edited all portions of the manuscript, and conducted library research, often on short notice.

I extend appreciation to friend and former student Rebecca Kaiser, Colusa County Schools, who contributed five exciting and practical LEs to chapters 8 and 9. Lisa Carpenter and Brenda Anglin provided excellent editing and typing during the early stages of the manuscript. I want to thank my friend Peggy Gray for her encouragement and manuscript preparation. Department Chair Don Chu, always looking for ways to generate scholarship, provided financial and moral support throughout the writing of this book.

I would like to acknowledge two past mentors. Dr. Bill Larson, University of Southern Mississippi, deserves special recognition for giving a rookie professor the chance to grow and learn in higher education. Teacher and coach Bill Turner taught me the importance of humility, persistence, a strong work ethic, and skill practice.

I extend appreciation to the children and teachers from two elementary schools: Sacred Heart School, Hattiesburg, Mississippi, and Notre Dame School, Chico, California. For the past 16 years these children have allowed me to learn from them, experiment with content and methods, and train numerous teachers of whom I am very proud.

Last, a special thanks to Scott Wikgren, Christine Hopple, and Julia Anderson from Human Kinetics Publishers. Scott has always encouraged my work. Christine and Julia, as content editors, provided careful and helpful suggestions to greatly improve this manuscript. Thanks for your patience and support.

Part I

Developmentally Appropriate Movement Concepts and Skills

In 1992 the National Association for Sport and Physical Education (NASPE) published a document entitled *Developmentally Appropriate Physical Education Practices for Children*. The document, developed by the executive committee of the Council on Physical Education for Children (COPEC), represents the collective wisdom of many physical educators about what good elementary physical education is. The principles NASPE espoused in this document guided the development of this and the other four books in this series.

Part I begins with an overview of developmentally appropriate movement concepts and motor skills, why they should be part of a quality elementary PE program, and how this approach differs from what has been traditionally taught in physical education. Chapter 1 also includes a definition of the physically educated person, including psychomotor, cognitive, and affective objectives, and a discussion of the significance of this definition for children's movement concepts and motor skills instruction.

Virtually no two teaching situations are identical in physical education. Chapter 2 provides several suggestions on how you can structure your program to fit the idiosyncrasies of your school.

This chapter includes ideas for teaching lessons with limited space, equipment, and time. As explained in this chapter, quality programs can be developed in less-than-ideal situations, but it's not easy.

A complete description of the content, including definitions of terms specific to the content area, is provided in chapter 3. As you review the content of all five books, you will quickly see that they contain much more than fun games and activities that are designed simply to keep children occupied for 30 minutes or so. Each content area outlines a developmentally appropriate curriculum designed to provide children with a logical progression of tasks leading to skillfulness in, and enjoyment of, physical activity.

Chapter 4 describes and discusses the key teaching principles that are used to provide developmentally appropriate experiences for children. This chapter applies pedagogical principles as they relate specifically to teaching the content included in the book. As you know, each of the five content areas has unique characteristics that master teachers are aware of as they teach their lessons.

The final chapter in Part I is on assessment. It describes practical ways to assess how well

1

children are learning the concepts and skills related to the content being taught. As we enter the 21st century, educators are increasingly being required to document, in realistic ways, the progress their children are making. This requirement presents unique challenges to the elementary school physical educator who may teach 600 or more children each week. Chapter 5 provides some realistic suggestions for ways to formatively assess what children are learning.

Chapter 1

Why Is It Important to Teach Children Movement Concepts and Skills?

I vividly remember my elementary school experiences when I was growing up in Virginia. Chalk dust covered the blackboard, and the desks were arranged in groups to form learning teams in Mrs. Quigg's fourth-grade class. Mrs. Quigg was serious about teaching and learning and held high expectations for each child. She was a talented elementary teacher who continually encouraged her class and convinced me that I was capable of learning math, science, reading, or whatever subject we studied. I recall the grown-up feeling of being a school patrol; the gigantic playground with monkey bars and swings; the blacktop where four-square, basketball, and kickball were played; the unkempt softball diamond with cardboard bases; the blue biography section of the library; and the multipurpose "cafetorium." Those were some of the best of my 40 years.

I was viewed as a leader when we played competitive games and sports; when teams were chosen I was usually a first- or second-round pick. Looking back, my motor skills were forever changing and improving because I practiced so much. It was important to me to move, to run fast, to model myself after the professional players of the day. For most students recess and physical education were the dessert in the curriculum, but they were my entree.

Mr. Wheeler, our itinerant physical education specialist, was probably the most popular teacher in the school. After all, he taught us games, dances, sports, and relays 30 minutes each week. Mr. Wheeler was tall, wore glasses, was balding, and taught in black high-top sneakers. He seemed old at the time. His energy level was high, and he knew how to motivate children on the playground.

Because of my interest in sports, when I was a fourth grader Mr. Wheeler asked me to participate in the afterschool intramural program. Intramurals—for *boys* in grades five and six—included competitive wrestling and basketball. I remember the 8-foot basketball goals in the cafetorium that made the sport easier for growing players and the competitive intramural leagues with referees. For me the enjoyment of playing far outweighed winning and losing. I developed a consistent hook shot and learned to shoot with my nondominant hand. In retrospect, I see that I was considered athletic because of what I had learned from my older peers.

Many of my friends were not as proficient at performing sport skills. My friend Tish struggled throughout his school years in physical education. He always wanted to be picked first, win races, and perform better. This I know because of our talks on the playground. I can recall helping him during a third-grade kickball game. I suggested that he run toward the moving ball and make contact with it at his shoelaces; the technique usually worked well for me. He and I both smiled when he landed on second base after lofting the ball to the outfield. Had Tish been faster he would have tripled. His fielding was often hindered by a fear of being hit in the face. Nevertheless, my tip about kicking bonded our relationship; it was probably my incipient teaching experience in physical education.

By today's standards, Mr. Wheeler's program could be characterized as traditional. The focus was on the immediacy of fun, competition, and a release or break in the weekly learning schedule. It met the needs of some children, particularly those who had developed motor skills outside of class. Mr. Wheeler's program was probably acceptable 30 years ago even if Tish never learned how to catch, because we didn't know then what we do today about how children acquire motor skills. Today we have a solid base of research and theory to help us design physical education programs for all children. Programs today could meet Tish's needs by providing frequent opportunities for skill practice, teacher instruction and analysis, and specific feedback.

For the past three decades researchers at the universities of Wisconsin, Indiana, and South Carolina, Michigan State, Ohio State, Virginia Tech, and other schools have been studying children and teachers in physical education. We know better what and how to teach. We have a body of knowledge about motor development, exercise physiology, pedagogy, motor learning, and biomechanics (Gallahue, 1989; Graham, Holt/Hale, & Parker, 1993; Haubenstricker & Seefeldt, 1986; Magill, 1989; Roberton & Halverson, 1984; Siedentop, 1991). This body of knowledge can make positive differences in the lives of children.

We should be applying the theories, the results of research, and the best practices available to our programs so that children become physically educated. Today's elementary programs should

no longer resemble the one I remember. If they do, we are miseducating children. If traditional games, sports, and dances combined with dubious methodology comprise the elementary curriculum, these programs exist for the wrong reasons.

I have four objectives for this first chapter. First, I discuss the purposes of elementary physical education in relation to current thinking by members of the National Association for Sport and Physical Education and the Council on Physical Education for Children. Second, I disclose three false assumptions that often hold back teachers and children in physical education classes. Third, I outline the content for teaching movement concepts and motor skills. Finally, I provide a rationale for teaching students the movement alphabet before they participate in advanced games, dance, gymnastics, and physical fitness activities.

Purposes of Elementary Physical Education

What are the "right" reasons behind elementary physical education? Experts with various viewpoints have offered numerous purposes. Most of them center on cognitive, affective, and psychomotor learning. The following five purposes, reshaped from Schurr (1975), keep me focused on the children and teachers with whom I work. Moreover, these purposes clarify the importance of this subject matter in the elementary curriculum. Developmentally appropriate programs should help children become aware of their movement potential, move competently and confidently, understand and apply the movement fundamentals, become versatile movers, and value healthy play.

Become Aware of Movement Potential

All children we teach must be encouraged to explore their abilities. As parents and teachers we don't know a child's potential or limitations. Because of maturational differences and uneven learning opportunities it is nearly impossible to predict a child's rate of motor development.

One recent spring I taught 30 second graders at Notre Dame School a lesson on throwing. The lesson's focus was overhand throwing. Each child was to throw a tennis ball against the wall and make a catch on the rebound. One child, Terry, sat down and crossed his arms and legs, obviously upset after several minutes of skill practice. I asked Terry why he was sitting instead of throwing. He said, "Mr. Butcher [sic], I'm no good at this. I'm just not athletic." Surprised at his response—not his skill level—I countered, "Terry, you haven't been on the earth long enough to get good at anything yet. Let's move up; I'll watch you throw and see if I can help. We can worry later about who is and is not athletic." This little episode illustrates a common scenario among children—Terry was afraid to fail and was feeling left behind by the other children (see Figure 1.1). More important, he labeled himself unathletic, a clear reflection of the pressures adults impose on children to grow up quickly and learn quickly (Elkind, 1988).

We do not know who of today's youngsters will become the athletes, musicians, clerks, doctors, engineers, lawyers, and artists of the world. It's OK for children to be where they are. A specialist's job is teaching children, whatever their levels, and bringing out the movement potential within each of them.

Move Competently and Confidently

As they move in work or play, children should feel capable, not flawed or awkward. Self-esteem is tied to feeling comfortable, understanding what to do, and sensing acceptance from peers in a physical education class. Gallahue (1989)

suggests that "the concept children have of themselves is based on their feelings about themselves and what they think others think of them" (p. 369). Children who develop competent motor skills grow in confidence, which can lead to further participation (Romance, 1985). Educators believe some children can develop a self-defeating cycle if they don't exceed rudimentary skill levels or if the performance of motor task components becomes arrested at early developmental levels (Roberton & Halverson, 1984).

In my experience, a majority of children lack the necessary competence in movement to feel good about participating in traditional physical education classes. These children need assurance that they can handle the unpredictable situations arising in a dynamic environment. When children become skillful, they leave class thinking "I can do that pretty well" or "I may not be great but I can hold my own."

We must remember that physical education takes place in public: Children witness their peers' successes and failures. They typically keep one eye on their peers, noticing the varied responses to movement tasks. Some look for ideas to help learn a movement, while others check to see who is "cool" or taking the challenges seriously. This is not the case with many cognitive tasks. When children read, write themes, or compute with numbers, they usually work independently. When children are engaged in games and sports, they often are aware of who makes the last out, which team is behind, and who knocks in

Figure 1.1   Encourage children to explore their abilities.

the winning run. Teachers should help children focus on the learning process, rather than the product, during initial stages of learning. Furthermore, teachers must observe and be prepared to raise a child's level of competence and confidence in moving (Allison, 1985; Barrett, 1985; Bressan & Weiss, 1982).

Understand and Apply Movement Fundamentals

Like a language, physical education has a structure. Knowing about and practicing fundamental movement concepts and motor skills is prerequisite to more advanced learning games, sports, dance, gymnastics, and fitness. These fundamentals lay the foundation for many adolescent and adult activities. Learning these fundamentals is the cornerstone for a developmentally appropriate physical education program.

Become Versatile Movers

Children should learn to become all-around movers during the primary and intermediate years. For example, a 3-week unit on throwing and catching can provide numerous opportunities for children to practice these important motor skills. Throwing and catching will eventually be applied to sports and games, but it is not necessary to play softball or football to acquire these important skills.

Mastery of basic movement concepts and motor skills can free children to attempt specialized and complex movements later in more dynamic and structured environments. Some younger children will be ready for specialization, but most will not. Although we should remember depth and breadth in designing programs, during the early years let's encourage children to be more generalists than specialists. Although an effective classroom teacher would not limit the class to reading fiction, some physical education teachers tend to narrow the curriculum by assigning only the culture's most popular sports and games.

Value Healthy Play

Children should begin to recognize the relationship between feeling good and regular activity, diet, and stress reduction. Hopefully, children will begin to value regular activity and choose to fill time outside of school in physically active ways. The elementary school years should strengthen a child's innate love of play and provide the foundation for future physical education experiences in secondary school and adulthood.

The Physically Educated Child

Would you know a physically educated child by observation of motor skills and physical fitness scores or by interviewing teachers, friends, and parents? The National Association for Sport and Physical Education (Franck et al., 1991) has defined the physically educated person, and it is worthwhile to examine how its definition applies to children (see Figure 1.2).

Outcomes statements in each of the five categories (*Has* learned skills . . . ; *Is* physically fit . . . ; *Does* physical activity regularly . . . ; *Knows* the implications and benefits . . . ; and *Values* physical activity . . .) can be used as guides in designing a developmentally appropriate program for elementary school children. Outcomes 1 to 3, 6, 13, 17, and 20 have special significance for children learning movement concepts and motor skills.

This NASPE definition of the physically educated person complements the purposes of elementary physical education. In helping children become aware of movement, teachers challenge them to explore the body's capacity in a variety of manipulative, locomotor, and nonlocomotor skills. When teachers set positive expectations for competence and confidence in movement concepts and motor skills, they move students toward achieving mature motor skills and patterns. When teachers foster understanding and application of concepts, they communicate the benefits of physical activity. When teachers emphasize versatility, they promote competence in different forms of physical activity. Finally, when teachers impart the value of healthy play, they demonstrate the contributions of physical activity to a healthy lifestyle.

One additional feature of NASPE's interest in developmentally appropriate physical education has been to identify sample, noninclusive competencies or benchmarks specific to every other grade level (see Figure 1.3). These goals help teachers assess a child's progress toward becoming physically educated. I will refer to these benchmarks for children in grades K through 6 in presenting objectives and learning experiences.

Reflective teachers will notice that the words *has*, *knows*, and *values* directly address the three domains of learning (psychomotor, cognitive, and

A Physically Educated Person

- **Has** learned skills necessary to perform a variety of physical activities:
  1. Moves using concepts of body awareness, space awareness, effort, and relationships
  2. Demonstrates competence in a variety of manipulative, locomotor, and nonlocomotor skills
  3. Demonstrates competence in combinations of manipulative, locomotor, and nonlocomotor skills performed individually and with others
  4. Demonstrates competence in many different forms of physical activity
  5. Demonstrates proficiency in a few forms of physical activity
  6. Has learned how to learn new skills

- **Is** physically fit:
  7. Assesses, achieves, and maintains physical fitness
  8. Designs safe, personal fitness programs in accordance with principles of training and conditioning

- **Does** participate regularly in physical activity:
  9. Participates in health-enhancing physical activity at least three times a week
  10. Selects and regularly participates in lifetime physical activities

- **Knows** the implications of and the benefits from involvement in physical activities:
  11. Identifies the benefits, costs, and obligations associated with regular participation in physical activity
  12. Recognizes the risk and safety factors associated with regular participation in physical activity
  13. Applies concepts and principles to the development of motor skills
  14. Understands that wellness involves more than being physically fit
  15. Knows the rules, strategies, and appropriate behaviors for selected physical activities
  16. Recognizes that participation in physical activity can lead to multicultural and international understanding
  17. Understands that physical activity provides the opportunity for enjoyment, self-expression, and communication

- **Values** physical activity and its contribution to a healthful lifestyle:
  18. Appreciates the relationships with others that result from participation in physical activity
  19. Respects the role that regular physical activity plays in the pursuit of lifelong health and well-being
  20. Cherishes the feelings that result from regular participation in physical activity

---

Figure 1.2 Outcomes of quality physical education programs. *Note.* The "Physically Educated Person" document containing these outcomes and accompanying benchmarks (see Figure 1.3) can be obtained by contacting NASPE, 1900 Association Dr., Reston, VA 22091-1599 or by calling 1-800-321-0789.
From *Physical Education Outcomes: A Project of the National Association for Sport and Physical Education* by M. Franck, G. Graham, H. Lawson, T. Loughrey, R. Ritson, M. Sanborn, and V. Seefeldt (the Outcomes Committee of NASPE), 1991. Reprinted by permission of the National Association for Sport and Physical Education, Reston, VA.

affective). The criteria *is* physically fit and *does* participate regularly also complement the psychomotor domain. A fit child is better able to perform and master the movement concepts and motor skills. Regular vigorous participation in a variety of movements demonstrates to a child that movement patterns are part of life.

We teach children first and subject matter second: Elementary specialists espouse this philosophy of the whole child in physical education, yet many fall woefully short in designing specific lessons, neglecting the cognitive and affective domains. Even though skillful movement and fitness are primary concerns of physical education,

intellectual, social, and attitudinal changes in children can be part of a plan (Buschner, 1989, 1990; Griffin, 1982; Hellison & Templin, 1991; Masser, 1990). These learning domains should mesh as children participate in physical education.

Debunking False Assumptions About Physical Education

Having developed a better understanding of what it means for a child to be physically educated, teachers should examine a few false assumptions that have hindered children's physical education during the past 30 years.

As a result of participating in a quality physical education program, it is reasonable to expect that the student will be able to do the following:

Psychomotor Domain (Has, Is, Does)

Demonstrate clear contrasts between fast and slow speeds as they travel (K, #3)

Distinguish between straight, curved, and zigzag pathways while traveling in various ways (K, #4)

Travel, demonstrating a variety of relationships with objects (e.g., over, under, behind, alongside, through) (K, #6)

Place a variety of body parts into high, medium, and low levels (K, #7)

Demonstrate the difference between an overhand and an underhand throw (K, #11)

Continuously jump a swinging rope held by others (K, #13)

Form round, narrow, wide, and twisted body shapes alone and with a partner (K, #14)

Throw a ball hard, demonstrating an overhand technique, a side orientation, and opposition (1-2, #10)

Catch, using properly positioned hands, a gently thrown ball (1-2, #11)

Skip, hop, gallop, and slide using a mature motor pattern (1-2, #18)

While traveling, avoid or catch an individual or object (3-4, #1)

Leap, leading with either foot (3-4, #2)

Hand dribble and foot dribble a ball and maintain control while traveling within a group (3-4, #5)

Consistently strike a softly thrown ball with a bat or paddle, demonstrating an appropriate grip, side to the target, and swing plane (3-4, #7)

Develop patterns and combinations of movements into repeatable sequences (3-4, #8)

Cognitive Domain (Knows)

Identify selected body parts, skills, and movement concepts (K, #18)

Recognize similar movement concepts in a variety of skills (1-2, #23)

Identify ways movement concepts can be used to refine movement skills (3-4, #21)

Design games, dance, and gymnastics sequences that are personally interesting (3-4, #26)

Affective Domain (Values)

Identify feelings that result from participation in physical activity (K, #22)

Accept the feelings resulting from challenges, successes, and failures in physical activity (1-2, #28)

Appreciate differences and similarities in others' physical activity (3-4, #27)

Figure 1.3 Sample benchmarks relevant for movement concepts and motor skills. The first number in parentheses following each benchmark relates to the grade level that benchmark can be found under in the NASPE document; the second number gives the specific benchmark for that grade level. These will be referenced to objectives for the learning experiences in Part II of this text, when appropriate. See page 57 for further information.

From *Physical Education Outcomes: A Project of the National Association for Sport and Physical Education* by M. Franck, G. Graham, H. Lawson, T. Loughrey, R. Ritson, M. Sanborn, and V. Seefeldt (The Outcomes Committee of NASPE), 1991. Adapted by permission of the National Association for Sport and Physical Education, Reston, VA.

Learning How to Move Develops Naturally Through Maturation

This assumption holds true only when referring to a normally developing infant's reflexes, reactions, and rudimentary movements during the first 2 years of life (Gallahue, 1989; Haubenstricker & Seefeldt, 1986; Haywood, 1986; Payne & Isaacs, 1991; Thomas, 1984). Most toddlers can learn to crawl, creep, walk, and run without adult intervention.

Proficiency in any motor skill, however, requires the opportunity, practice, feedback, and encouragement that teachers and a well-designed program can provide. We should not assume that children already know how to walk, run, throw, or catch. They may have attempted these motor skills, but that is no guarantee of mastering them or being able to perform them under a wide variety of conditions (Higgins, 1991). Furthermore, genetics and gender are usually ancillary factors: For prepubescent children most gender-related differences in motor skill and fitness are learned, not determined by physiological and psychological causes (Thomas, J., Lee, & Thomas, K., 1988).

Most Children Are Skilled Enough to Engage in Advanced Sports, Games, and Dances

Teaching standard sports, games, dances, and adult exercise routines produces failure with most children at the elementary level. Far too many children never surpass the "initial and elementary stages" (Gallahue, 1989) or the "precontrol and control levels of skill proficiency" (Graham et al., 1993). Children and teachers are easily fooled into believing that kicking and sliding have been learned, only to see these skills break down during soccer games.

Ask second graders "Are you a good kicker?" and most of them will answer yes, believing also that they can read, write, and add. But can they? They may assume, erroneously, that because they have tried these skills they have learned them. Evidence is clear, however, that children are not acquiring sufficient motor skills for later life (Graham, 1987). Teachers should not permit pressure from students to substitute for professional judgment for readiness to learn advanced skills. Master teachers should know when children are ready.

Learning Basic Skills Does Not Motivate Children

Many instructors, parents, and administrators assume that teaching basic skills creates boredom and even antipathy to physical education. Some believe that basic skills are too difficult to teach and that physical education should only be fun. In many schools this erroneous notion degrades physical education to a position of supervised recreation. Recreation is important, but it should not be confused with instruction designed to change the psychomotor, cognitive, and affective behaviors of children in a systematic fashion. Equating unstructured play and even supervised recreation with physical education minimizes its contribution as an academic class where learning is carefully planned, implemented, and evaluated. Keeping children "busy, happy, and good" can easily appear to supersede learning (Placek, 1983).

Working with a developmental curriculum (Graham et al., 1987), I would argue, increases student motivation and decreases boredom when teachers design lessons that are appropriate to the skill and development of individual children. Planning this way is more time-consuming than selecting a few games each week, and teachers

must carefully observe children move. The benefits, however, far outweigh the costs in time and preparation. It may be easier to roll out the ball and teach the way we were taught, but it is professionally irresponsible to call this physical education. Moreover, fun is a by-product in a developmentally appropriate program, not a goal in itself. Children enjoy learning that meets their needs, whether in reading, writing, math, or physical education.

Learning the Movement Alphabet

During the elementary school years children learn formal language. Reading and writing are basic skills that all children must acquire as a foundation for further learning and functioning in an information society. Typically students first learn to identify and recite the alphabet; then they discover that these letters can be arranged into words and that words in turn will form sentences communicating meaning. Third-grade children combine sentences to form paragraphs that may culminate in a letter to a friend or an essay on some subject of interest. Clear thinking and writing come only after practicing and mastering the alphabet.

In elementary physical education we too have an alphabet that requires mastery. Instead of 26 letters there are 12 movement concepts and 18 motor skills that should be carefully practiced and understood before sport, game, dance, gymnastics, and exercise applications. These movement concepts and motor skills can be considered *organizing centers*, logical themes or concepts that unify content in a sequential and progressive way (Melograno, 1979). Kicking, for example, is within the organizing center of motor skills' manipulative patterns.

Motor skills are the action words or verbs (e.g., the fifth graders will *kick* the ball). *Movement concepts* are the adverbs that modify the motor skills (e.g., the children will run in a *zigzag pathway*). Movement concepts help a child modify the movement sequence, depending upon the task. These concepts can become the entire focus of a lesson (see chapters 6 and 7). The motor skills and movement concepts are listed in Table 1.1.

Graham et al. (1993) call the alphabet *movement concepts and skill themes*. Other authors classify it as fundamental locomotor and nonlocomotor skills, stability movements, movement awareness, movement education skills and concepts, perceptual awareness, and manipulatives

Table 1.1   The Movement Alphabet

Motor skills—verbs		Movement concepts—adverbs			
Locomotor patterns	Manipulative patterns	Body awareness	Space awareness	Effort	Relationships
Walking	Throwing	Body parts	General space	Speed	Objects or others
Jogging/	Catching	Shapes	Self-space	Force	Partner
running	Kicking	Curved	Directions	Flow	
Hopping	Punting	Twisted	Levels		
Skipping	Dribbling with feet	Narrow	Pathways		
Galloping	Dribbling with	Wide	Extensions		
Leaping	hands	Symmetrical			
Chasing	Striking	Asymmetrical			
Dodging	Volleying	Nonlocomotor movements			
Fleeing		Swing and sway			
Faking		Twist and turn			
Jumping and		Bend and curl			
landing		Stretch			
Sliding		Sink			
		Push and pull			
		Shake			
		Base of support			

(Gabbard, LeBlanc, & Lowy, 1987; Gallahue, 1989; Kirchner, 1992; Nichols, 1986; Thomas et al., 1988). Like common letter combinations (*er, ing, th, st, ed, pr*), many movement forms require two or more concepts or actions: catching and throwing; running, jumping, and landing; directions and pathways; and time and force. These movement forms are ever-changing as children engage in dynamic games and sports.

Many physical education programs minimize the teaching of movement concepts and motor skills, including them only as cursory units within the curriculum. Placing these basics at the center of study in pre-K to sixth grade is more appropriate and teaches children that movement concepts and motor skills are the stuff of advanced performance. I would classify physical education into sequential stages, with Stage I being the alphabet. Just as students recite the ABCs, they should master each of the movement concepts and motor skills before entering middle or junior high school (see Figure 1.4).

Acquiring skills is a gradual process, and the content offered in Stages II and III develops continually from Stage I. With most beginners competence and confidence will not accompany such complex movements as basketball and ballet. The combinations of concepts and skills used in a dynamic variety of activities are beyond the

movement literacy of most elementary school children. Knowing that some adults would fail complex movement sequences tells me that children would have great difficulty learning basketball without first understanding the alphabet of movement.

Skill acquisition follows practice under a variety of conditions and combinations using the alphabet of movement. A developmentally appropriate program provides the necessary transition from movement concepts and motor skills (Stage I) to movement contexts (Stage II) and complex movements (Stage III). My premise is that we don't rush children to Stage III in physical education, language arts, or mathematics! Just as we would not ask a first grader to read *War and Peace*, we should not rush that child to play basketball.

Rationale for the Movement Alphabet

The old adage "you must walk before you run" implies the progression in learning. In his "schema theory" Richard A. Schmidt (1988) suggests that practicing generic movements under a variety of conditions increases subsequent ability to learn new movements and sport skills. In

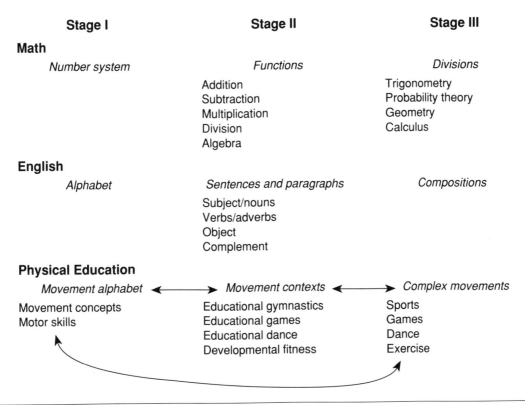

Figure 1.4   Stages of developmentally appropriate learning.

other words, a wide base of movement experiences helps children retrieve and combine learned movement patterns.

Motor development involves both heredity and environmental factors throughout one's lifespan (Gallahue, 1989; Payne & Isaacs, 1991). There is some speculation that the quality of adult life is affected in part by the movement experiences learned during the elementary years (Haubenstricker & Seefeldt, 1986). Thomas et al. (1988) have identified two reasons why motor skills are important:

> First, children and adults are more likely to participate in activities if they have enough skill to enjoy some success. Second, by participating in these movement activities, they not only enjoy successful movement experiences, but they move vigorously for extended periods of time, which contributes to the objective of developing physical fitness. (p. 37)

Other motor development models support the notion of progression and stages of motor skill acquisition (Gallahue, 1982; Seefeldt, 1979), explaining in linear fashion how development occurs and in what sequence. Research on com-

monly used motor skills has demonstrated how children progress through various stages, or levels (Gallahue, 1989; Graham et al., 1993; Stanley, 1977; Wickstrom, 1977). Whatever the terminology describing motor skill acquisition, researchers know that children exhibit predictable motor skill stages and can improve through quality physical education programs. Using these theories about stages of motor skill and the movement alphabet seemingly would have allowed my friend Tish to become a more skillful mover.

Physical education specialists must focus on the qualitative aspects of helping children perform basic skills (Rink, 1985). As George Graham (1987) suggests, some physical educators have failed children and youth in the area of motor skill acquisition:

> Watch a class of high school students playing softball. Notice how many of them throw overhand improperly. . . . There is no anatomical or biomechanical reason why they can't throw correctly. They just haven't learned, even though they may have attended physical education classes for six or seven years! . . . Students have been exposed to the correct way of throwing, but haven't learned to throw correctly. (p. 46)

Youth Sports and Stage III Activities

Is it a physical educator's job to move all children to a Stage III competitive sport setting? Sport leagues attempt to provide youths with opportunities to participate in active physical learning, but not all of them are successful in considering children's needs. Most youth sport organizations are based on a scaled down adult participation model. In many parts of the U.S. parents seem to believe that youth leagues are a worthy proxy for quality physical education. They view youth sports as synonymous in content and process with physical education programs.

Telling me that half of the children participating in the spring league would not return for a second year of play, my son's youth soccer coach proceeded to point out which children he believed would drop out of the league. During practices and games he observed that the children who lacked skill, knowledge, and fitness often showed the least interest. The coach's predictions were accurate.

Youth sports are not a substitute for quality physical education in the schools; the specialized training they provide helps primarily those children with the highest interest and ability. Syndicated columnist Dave Barry (1990) gives a humorous, yet poignant, account of Little League baseball.

> To participate in this highly popular sport, all you need to do is get a small child who would be infinitely happier just staying home and playing in the dirt, and put a uniform on this child and make him stand for hours out on the field with other reluctant children who are no more capable of hitting or catching or accurately throwing a baseball than they are of performing neurosurgery. (pp. 131-132)

Little League baseball—or teaching complex sports similarly in physical education—is in-appropriate for most children who have a limited movement vocabulary and immature motor skills in throwing, catching, running, striking, and dodging. We want to encourage competence and confidence at the child's actual level, not confuse a student with quick advancement to Stage III activities and youth sports. Save youth sports for children who are ready to enjoy the specialization, competition, and fun they can provide.

Summary

As an elementary student I felt it was important to run, skip, throw, catch, and kick. Children in the 1990s are no different. They want to become skillful and feel good about their physical abilities. Many children hope to apply their skills outside of the school setting. However, many of our physical education programs do not teach much more than 20 fun games. We need no longer use a traditional 1960s curriculum model when our understanding of how children acquire motor skills, knowledge, and positive attitudes has advanced. Poorly designed programs yield children who lack motor skill, exhibit low fitness levels, and dislike or avoid physical activity.

To help children learn skills teachers should have clear purposes, an understanding of the physically educated child, and a sound theoretical background to design developmentally appropriate programs. Furthermore, teachers should view with skepticism assumptions about what children learn in physical education. This will require questioning traditional beliefs, intuition, and personal experience.

All children can become aware of their movement potential, achieve competence and confidence, and value healthy play if they learn the movement alphabet, movement concepts, and motor skills. These are prerequisites to sports, educational games, dance, gymnastics, and fitness. This alphabet provides a unifying structure for a developmental approach and is the cornerstone for complex motor skills.

Chapter 2

Tailoring Movement Concepts and Skills to Fit Your Teaching Situation

Teaching would be much easier if all schools and all grade levels were identical. Then a standardized curriculum with detailed lesson plans would work everywhere. The fact is, however, that our teaching situations have some similarities—and some definite differences! These differences include class size, equipment, facilities, class frequency, length of the class period, a broad range of ages, abilities, and special needs within the same class of children, and the community.

During my first year of teaching as an elementary specialist, I tried to design a curriculum centered on the movement concepts and motor skills. I had my undergraduate course textbook (Schurr, 1975), class notes, a good list of library references, student teaching experience, and lots of ambition. The school provided a cafetorium to use from 8:00 to 11:00 and 1:00 to 3:15, two spacious blacktops, a large grassy field, enough manipulative equipment to give each two children one item (e.g., 15 jump ropes for 30 children), and classes not exceeding 35 children. I taught 430 children two times a week: not utopia but a manageable situation for teaching physical education.

My colleagues in the school district were less fortunate. Many of them taught classes of 70, meeting the children once a week and struggling to learn the names of nearly 900 children before the holidays. Teachers often feel as though they are observing a sea of children; 20 children in motion seem like 40, and 40 seem like 80 (see Figure 2.1).

Figure 2.1 Teachers sometimes feel as if they face a sea of children.

We all have spent many hours collecting plastic milk cartons, making beanbags and hula hoops, and searching for ways to raise money for more gymnastics equipment. Early in our careers we learned the necessity of adapting the curriculum to match the teaching environment. This chapter briefly describes some ways both novice and veteran teachers can adapt the movement alphabet to various teaching situations to best meet the needs of the children and also to heighten their enjoyment and learning (see Figure 2.2).

Class Size

Although it is recommended that "physical education classes contain the same number of children as the classrooms (e.g., 25 children per class)" (Council on Physical Education for Children, 1992), some schools and districts schedule two or three classes at the same time, which means the PE teacher must teach 60 or more children simultaneously. Although this makes the teacher's job difficult, there are ways that teachers can develop the content to provide children with positive (albeit far from ideal) learning experiences. For example, the use of stations, or learning centers, is probably one of the more efficient ways to organize large groups of children (Graham, 1992). And using written directions can minimize the time spent talking to the children, who often seem less inclined to listen when they are in large groups. Also, the teacher must devote substantial time to teaching management routines (Siedentop, 1991) or protocols (Graham, 1992) so that classes are run efficiently with minimal interruptions.

Equipment

One reason why large class sizes are *not* recommended is that most physical education programs do not have sufficient equipment—not even for 25 or 30 children. Stock for many schools today includes a bat; a softball; four each of bases, hurdles, basketballs, kickballs, playground balls, and hula hoops; several jump ropes (tangled in a knot); a record player donated by the music teacher; and assorted recordings of fun things to do with the parachute, hula hoops, or lummi sticks. No wonder that in most parts of the United States physical education lacks developmental standards. Duck, Duck, Goose; kickball; and relays endure. Consequently, if teachers are not careful, the children spend considerable time waiting for turns rather than actually moving. But innovative teachers have discovered ways to maximize practice opportunities for children, even with limited equipment.

The essential equipment for children to learn the movement alphabet includes a record or tape player, drum or tambourine, hula hoops, carpet squares, jump ropes, balloons, plastic bats, hockey sticks, milk cartons, traffic cones,

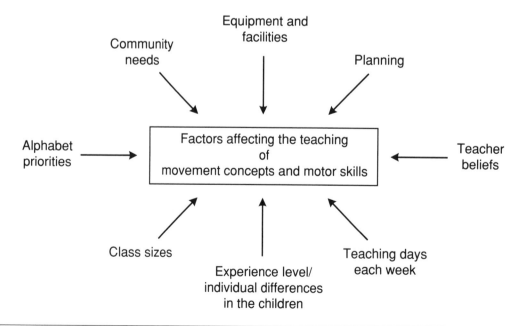

Figure 2.2   Factors affecting the teaching of movement concepts and motor skills.

paddles, and balls of different shapes and sizes. First among this equipment is the drum; my students and friends believe that I cannot teach without it. Furthermore, as I design developmental taxonomies for the motor skills (see Figure 2.3) this list of equipment is only a beginning. Ideal programs have far more than these items. Using a little ingenuity, teachers can make much of the equipment for classes. The goal is for children to receive frequent practice opportunities, without fear of injury, and with minimal waiting time. Each teacher should adapt the facility and equipment in ways that help children become skillful.

Facilities

Although some teachers have adequate indoor and outdoor space, others are less fortunate. In fact, some teachers have no indoor space whatsoever. Others have no grassy areas. Following are some ideas and suggestions for how the content in this book can be adapted for limited indoor or outdoor space.

Ample play areas outdoors and indoors are helpful for teaching the movement alphabet. Plenty of grassy space is especially desirable for teaching running/jogging, chasing, fleeing, dodging, kicking, leaping, and jumping and landing. There are teachers in urban settings who would readily swap several basketball goals for a patch of grass. A floor or blacktop is not essential, but it is useful for practicing to dribble with hands or for when the ground is wet. Learning many locomotor and manipulative patterns works best in a space bounded by walls and blacktop. Eventually, children will want to confine movements in appropriate settings, such as tennis courts, baseball diamonds, and stages. A teacher should ask, Is there space enough here for each child to be safe when moving?

Many elementary schools have outdoor playground equipment that was designed historically to keep children busy and contented during recess. Instructional physical education was rare

in the 1950s and 1960s when most play equipment was constructed. The playground in my elementary school looks the same today as it did when I was a child. The basketball courts, tetherball pole, monkey bars, chinning bars, four-square lines, swings, teeter-totters, and basketball goals (same height as used in the NBA) apparently were designed by people who viewed elementary physical education as 20-fun-games-and-sports. Children often wonder why the basket is so high in the air. Adults, unfortunately, often forget what it was like to shoot for a basketball goal when they were four feet tall (see Figure 2.4). It's like riding on a DC3 racing against a Concorde.

Class Frequency and Length

Schools and classes differ in the number of days per week that the children attend physical education classes and the length of the classes. Children who have physical education every day for 30 minutes can be expected to learn more than children who have only 60 minutes of physical education each week. This is one reason it is virtually impossible to suggest a standardized physical education curriculum. As suggested in the section later in this chapter on planning, you will need to consider these factors as you plan. Aim to organize and teach your classes so that if students have physical education twice a week for 30 minutes, they receive more than 16 hours of actual learning time each year (Kelly, 1989).

Accommodating Individual Differences

Many classes today have children with special needs who are mainstreamed (i.e., their physical education class is scheduled with another class). In some instances you can accommodate children with special needs (not only those who are mainstreamed), by techniques such as *teaching by invitation* or *intratask variation* (Graham, 1992). In other instances it may be necessary to make

Catching Equipment

Balloons	Sock balls	Volleyballs	Basketballs
Beach balls	Paper balls	Footballs	Styrofoam art balls
Nerf balls	Kush balls	Tennis balls	Frisbees
Yarn balls	Playground balls (different sizes)	Soccer/kickballs	Boomerangs

Figure 2.3 Developmental equipment progression for catching.

Figure 2.4   Elementary facilities should be constructed with children in mind.

different adaptations to accommodate the needs of these students. Some accommodations that teachers can make for children when teaching movement concepts and motor skills are discussed in this section.

All children, even those who think they already know the rudimentary motor patterns, need plenty of practice with careful teacher observation and analysis to reach mature motor skill patterns. It is helpful to collect background information on each child, perhaps using an index card to record age, family situation, current academic progress, peer acceptance, and youth sport experiences. This information facilitates remembering children and planning learning experiences.

After you get a sense of the strengths and weaknesses in classes, it might be helpful to group students by their levels of experience in each category of the movement alphabet. One third-grade class will need lots of time to learn the locomotor skills or space awareness, while another class in the same school will be ready for combinations of locomotor and manipulative skills. A class of fifth graders that has only had recess or recreational games and sports may be more inexperienced than a third-grade class. As a rule of thumb, the majority of children in grades pre-K to 3 will be inexperienced, and though students in the intermediate grades will be more experienced, individual children demonstrate wide variations of skill.

With inexperienced classes it is best to isolate the motor skills and spend extra time stressing the movement concepts. I tend to address the whole class and make maximal use of the wall as a partner for teaching manipulative skills. I also make fewer equipment changes for the whole class during a lesson, provide more demonstrations of the motor skills, and rely heavily on pinpointing. Pinpointing lets the teacher select two or more children to demonstrate motor skills emphasizing cues, refinements, and creative solutions to problems (Graham, 1992).

With more experienced classes it is better to work more quickly through learning the motor skills. I tend to punctuate the movement concepts with more refined motor skills so they are observable. For example, striking with short implements is at a mature level when children can alter the movement by varying force, flow, level, and extension. The movement concepts are curricular threads to be revisited as motor skills improve.

My golf pro reminds me with unnerving frequency, to *swing*, rather than *hit*. Swinging at a stationary object requires the kinesthetic perception that only develops after comprehending and applying the concepts of timing, force, flow, direction, levels, pathways, and extensions during the movement. It is easy to see why so many people have difficulty breaking 100 playing golf. With experienced classes I tend to use more combinations of movement concepts and motor skills. The next step in physical education classes is to put these combinations into movement sequences that resemble the actions they will use for complex movements. Play-teach-play is most effective when children demonstrate more mature patterns (Graham, 1992). I rarely, if ever, stop to watch the children perform without using the opportunity to intervene and improve performance.

Community Needs

Another consideration is the characteristics of the community in which you teach. This includes not only the city or town but also the community of the school. Religious concerns may influence the content (e.g., some religions have prohibitions on dancing). In northern states ice skating or snow skiing may be part of the content to be taught. Some principals (who have yet to be fully educated about quality physical education) may have concerns about what content is (or is not) taught. Increasingly, for example, the safety of gymnastics is being questioned. Although I rarely have experienced misunderstandings about the motor skills, occasionally people in the community express reservations about the applications of the movement concepts behind dance. Teachers should strive to demonstrate the importance of the entire movement alphabet.

Planning

Chapter 3 contains an overview of the content that can be developed through the learning experiences in chapters 6 to 9. An important decision you must make as a teacher is how much of the content described in this book to use in your program. Remember, this is only one of five books (Belka, 1994; Purcell, 1994; Ratliffe & Ratliffe, 1994; Werner, 1994) that describe the content of physical education for children. Ideally, your program will include content from each of the areas, so you have some difficult decisions to make. A complete outline for planning is provided in *Teaching Children Physical Education* (Graham, 1992), but only you can develop the plans that will work best at your school. Also included in this book are benchmarks (Franck et al., 1991) that relate specifically to this content area. Use these benchmarks to help decide which aspects of the content are most important for your children to learn (see Figure 1.3).

Another important planning factor is the length of time you have taught the children. Your plans will (and should) be different for the first year of a program than for the tenth year. When you have worked with fifth and sixth graders from the time they started school, they will be able to do, and will know, different things than the fifth and sixth graders did your first year at that school.

Granting the importance of both movement concepts and motor skills, which are more important? Teachers never have enough time to develop mature patterns in all children. *Ideal* programs have 35 or fewer children per class and meet three or more times a week for 30 minutes; *inadequate* programs have more than 35 children per class and meet two or fewer times a week for 30 or fewer minutes. Ideal conditions, however, do not assure that the curriculum is valid and the teaching is effective. Likewise, inadequate conditions paradoxically can motivate teachers to produce quality programs that help students, despite the situational constraints.

If conditions are inadequate, careful planning is especially important to allocate time for particular letters of the movement alphabet. Just as the vowels are essential to language, while the letters x and z have more limited use, there are movement concepts and motor skills that should have priority. Graham (1992) provides a method to estimate "actual learning time" within any curriculum. Investing the energy to calculate actual learning time is probably a teacher's second important step in long term planning—after identifying goals and objectives. The actual learning time in a 2-days-per-week program is much less than it seems. Inadequate conditions can force teachers to make difficult curricular decisions. They must know what to include and what to postpone. The best gauge for making these decisions probably is what the children can do, but if you teach 500 children a week, their movement abilities may be less important than knowing who they are.

Thoughtful teachers can use the following division of the movement alphabet, based upon its broad application in games, sports, exercises, and dance. The *primary alphabet* includes the mandatory movement concepts and motor skills, even assuming inadequate conditions (see Table 2.1). The *secondary alphabet* contains the remainder of the movement concepts and motor skills (see Table 2.2). This division is not scientific, but based on my gut-level judgment after working with children and teachers for the past 17 years. Some parts of the primary alphabet can overlap the secondary list, if teachers know the content. For example, jumping and landing skills should aid in learning to hop. Hopping may be omitted in kindergarten but later included in grades 1, 3, and 5. Similarly, developing a mature throwing pattern will ultimately assist a student in learning to strike with short implements. The reason to consider dividing up the alphabet is unfortunate time constraints: What would happen if the classroom teacher could only use letters *A* through *L* because of time limitations in the classroom?

The best course for teachers working under inadequate conditions is to emphasize the primary alphabet and hope that proficiency in a limited number of skills will encourage children to supplement learning informally outside the gymnasium. There is little hope for education in schools that schedule a subject once every week or two. We implicitly declare that physical education is an appendage to the overall education there. Teachers who comply with such inadequate schedules encourage avoidance of physical

Table 2.1   Primary Alphabet

Body awareness	Space awareness	Effort	Relationships	Locomotor patterns	Manipulative patterns
Body parts	General space	Force	Objects or others	Jogging/running	Throwing
Shapes	Self-space			Leaping	Catching
Nonlocomotor movements	Directions			Jumping and landing	Kicking
Twist and turn	Levels			Sliding	Striking
Bend and curl					

Table 2.2   Secondary Alphabet

Body awareness	Space awareness	Effort	Relationships	Locomotor patterns	Manipulative patterns
Nonlocomotor movements	Pathways	Speed	Partner	Walking	Punting
Swing and sway	Extensions	Flow		Hopping	Dribbling with feet
Stretch				Skipping	Dribbling with hands
Sink				Galloping	Volleying
Push and pull				Chasing	
Shake				Dodging	
				Fleeing	

education, rather than positive educational changes. It's very simple: Minimal intervention has minimal impact.

Teachers who work under better conditions still should establish priorities in teaching the entire movement alphabet. The goal might be that all children be able to demonstrate a mature pattern in each of the locomotor and manipulative patterns. Children should have adequate time to revisit the movement alphabet over the 7 years of elementary school. They should be reaching the movement contexts (educational gymnastics, dance, games, and developmental fitness) as their skill levels and interests develop. Movement contexts apply the movement alphabet in dynamic settings.

Teacher Beliefs

A teacher's beliefs about children, the value of using the movement alphabet, teaching strategies, and class organization affect the quality and quantity of learning. Most veterans know that the key to effective teaching and coaching is to find ways to make practice tasks stimulating and even enjoyable. Graham (1992) suggests ways of motivating children to practice the motor skills, including videotaping, using individualized task sheets, teaching by invitation, and devising intratask variations.

Creative teaching uses both direct and indirect (inquiry) styles. Children learn the movement concepts best when they can experiment with problem-solving challenges. The motor skills also are learned more readily with a combination of direct and indirect approaches, using whole-class and station teaching (often in the same lesson). I use a massed or scattered teaching formation, with children finding their own work areas; I rarely form lines to practice the manipulative or locomotor skills and discourage university students from using lines to teach. The dynamic nature of movement requires control, with an awareness of space, people, and moving objects.

Summary

One of the most valid criticisms of physical education programs has been that they were designed only for athletes—and were a painful experience for those who were poorly skilled. Contemporary physical educators are moving away from the one-model-fits-all pattern of restrictive physical education toward programs that are adjusted, adapted, and designed specifically to match the abilities, interests, and needs of individual children. This chapter describes some of the considerations that contemporary teachers take into account when designing programs specifically for the children at their schools.

Chapter 3

Incorporating Movement Concepts and Skills Into Your Program

Each semester I invite college classes, adults who were elementary school children in the 1960s, 1970s, and 1980s, to recall their childhood physical education experiences. Most of them describe traditional programs, giving such examples as jump rope, parachute games, relays, sports and low-organized games, physical fitness testing, gymnastics, field days, square dance, kickball, and Bombardment. Their reminiscences are always more negative than positive: I have yet to hear prospective teachers describe movement-based or developmental experiences or say that the program taught running, dodging, throwing, kicking, or moving in different pathways—in essence, that they learned to move competently and confidently. Why is this? Despite recent conferences, workshops, textbooks, and curriculum guides, future teachers still remember physical education at the elementary level to be sports and whole-class games.

This chapter follows four objectives. First, it describes and differentiates the traditional and recommended developmental curriculum models for elementary physical education. Second, it clarifies the curricular content within each category of movement concepts and motor skills.

Third, it defines each movement concept and establishes what are mature patterns for each of the motor skills. Finally, this chapter offers critical components for teachers to focus on when teaching each of the motor skills.

Traditional Physical Education

What I consider traditional physical education is a program of balanced activities intended to emphasize equally sports and games, physical fitness, gymnastics, rhythm and dance, aquatics, and movement (see descriptions in Gentry, 1985; Kirchner, 1992; Thomas et al., 1988). Such a program allocates time for low-organized games and rhythmic activities at the primary level and for specialized sport skills and competition at the intermediate grades. This model is the cousin of multiactivity programs at the secondary level. Two- and 3-week units might include beanbags, hula hoops, the Electric Slide, soccer, and circuit training. When a teacher in a traditional program is asked what the children are learning the answer will be a specific activity: for example, rope jumping, the Virginia reel, or basketball.

In observing traditional programs in practice, I note the mutation I dub the 20-fun-games-and-sports curriculum (see Figure 3.1). Although strikingly similar to a recess-and-roll-out-the-ball model (Hellison & Templin, 1991), this model has several differences. It involves teaching a limited assortment of sports and games that are familiar to almost everyone from childhood, including such activities as Simon Says; Duck, Duck, Goose; whole-class kickball and dodgeball; softball; Four-Square; basketball; Hokey Pokey; square dance; physical fitness testing; calisthenics (Daily Dozen); track and field; soccer; flag football; and relays with some cosmetic variations.

In many elementary schools, the same activities are repeated in each grade because teachers believe children need and want them. These sports and games are the ones teachers learned as children and, in turn, pass along as a cultural heritage. Are they in the best and most appropriate interests of most children? Graham (1985) considered an important question when he asked whether any documentation showed that Duck, Duck, Goose is a good game for children.

Not for fitness certainly, hardly for skill development, but it may serve to enhance cooperation or as an enjoyable respite for six-year-olds from sitting at a desk. But do we know that Duck, Duck, Goose (or any game for that matter) enhances cooperation or enjoyment among children? . . . We don't have the evidence. It is blatantly non-existent in physical education. Up to this time, many school programs have been based more on testimonial, enthusiasm, personal beliefs, and the latest movie fad than on motor development, systematic documentation of learning, or field-based research. The fact is that there isn't a shred of evidence to support including Duck, Duck, Goose in the elementary school cur-

riculum. Yet it endures; oh, how it endures. (pp. 145-146)

My concern is that some teachers have developed a myopic view of elementary physical education based on early experience and they presume tradition breeds success. Their blurred vision of what comes beyond tomorrow's lesson, though satisfying the children's needs for fun, fails to see ahead to where children need to be in 5 to 10 years. Vision checks and corrective lenses, as necessary, should be mandatory before teaching physical education and every 3 years thereafter (Buschner, 1992). The place to start is examining the curriculum.

Curriculum Validity

The development of motor skills, physical fitness, knowledge, and positive values about physical education result from a good curriculum. Mention the term *curriculum* to experienced teachers and many of them shudder. A curriculum often seems too abstract because it includes everything teachers plan and implement, both explicitly and implicitly. Very simply, a curriculum is a long-term plan of learning experiences that follow a teacher's decisions about a curriculum model, organizing centers, objectives, content, methods, resources, and evaluation (see Figure 3.2). It includes *why* and *what* we teach. Like the human body's systems (muscular, respiratory, skeletal, etc.), all parts of the curriculum should work in concert to help children. Teachers should ask, Does my program have validity? Does it achieve the NASPE outcomes of a quality physical education program?

In discussing long-term planning, Graham (1992) asks what first graders should learn after 5 years of physical education to prepare them for adolescence and adulthood. Granted, this is a difficult question even for a veteran teacher; however, this kind of query helps teachers clarify a program's direction.

Duck, Duck, Goose	Hokey Pokey	Flag football
Whole-class kickball	Four-Square and handball	Basketball
Whole-class dodgeball	Animal stunts (Bear Crawl, Crab Walk, etc.)	Softball
Relays	Tumbling	Soccer
Simon Says	Performance-related fitness tests	Volleyball
Red Light, Green Light	Daily Dozen calisthenics	Square dance
Crows and Cranes	Track and field	

Figure 3.1 Twenty-fun-games-and-sports curriculum.

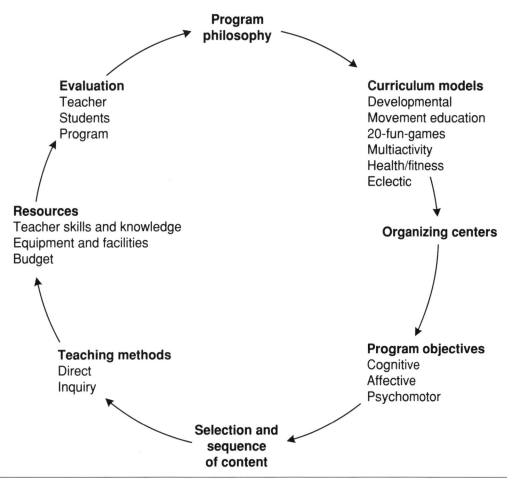

Figure 3.2 Systematic curriculum design.

Developmental Physical Education

For novice teachers, distinguishing between traditional, movement education, and developmental curriculum models is as difficult as drawing ideological lines between Republican, independent, and Democratic parties. Each of the models, in textbook form, holds to certain basic assumptions. The traditional model has been described. The movement education model, derived from Laban and Lawrence's (1947) framework, has evoked attention, misinterpretation, and marginal acceptance in the past 30 years. Its organizing centers include body awareness, spatial awareness, qualities of effort, and relationships. Proponents of movement education might design a series of lessons around themes such as force (light and heavy) or levels (high, medium, low) to help children understand and apply a knowledge of human movement (Barrett, 1985, 1988; Briggs, 1975; Gilliom, 1970;

Krueger, H., & Krueger, J.M., 1982; Logsdon et al., 1984; North, 1973; Stanley, 1977). Traditional units on softball, soccer, or physical fitness would be nonexistent using this model. Asking a teacher using the movement education approach what children are learning might elicit the response of space, time, and the flow of movement.

Developmentalists (Gabbard et al., 1987; Gallahue, 1989; Graham et al., 1993; Nichols, 1986; Thomas et al., 1988) espouse many of the philosophies and content of movement education but recognize the need for a parallel treatment of motor skills, including locomotor, nonlocomotor, and manipulative skills. Developmental physical education attempts to incorporate the stages of human learning in all three domains.

Research shows that for most motor skills there is a predictable sequence of learning. For example, we know that children can move through at least four stages in learning how to catch a ball. A child's developmental level for a particular task is contingent upon prior experience, interest, maturity, and ability rather than age, gender, or grade level. If a teacher using a developmental approach is asked what the children are learning, the response might be jumping and landing, striking, leaping, or creating symmetrical body shapes.

Bredekamp (1990) reminds us that "a major premise of developmentally appropriate practice is that each child is unique and has an individual pattern and timing of growth, as well as individual personality, learning style, and family background" (p. 65). For a program to be developmental, the learning process supersedes the product in the initial stages of acquiring a motor skill. This is a good principle to use with most elementary school children.

Each of the models emphasizes basic skills, but the organization and priorities of content, the scope, and the sequence of learning differ. A traditional curriculum model limits the amount of time and practice devoted to the movement concepts and motor skills. To compare curriculum models, an observer must read between the lines; some developmental programs may be traditional ones in disguise. For example, what essential concepts are children learning in units on parachutes and beanbags? Equipment is not content. Similarly, we don't teach tennis racket, hurdles, or softballs; these are tools that help children strike, jump and land, and throw and catch.

Be wary of programs that try to teach a smattering of every known activity: the eclectic model. Such programs often expose students to many activities at the expense of depth and mastery of the basics. Even if children receive 5 days of physical education each week with a specialist, the movement concepts and motor skills combined with educational games, dance, gymnastics, and fitness training (when children are ready) will be plenty to learn during the primary and intermediate years.

The first step in designing a developmentally appropriate curriculum is to understand the terminology associated with the movement concepts and motor skills. This alphabet is the foundation for motor learning.

The Movement Alphabet Revisited

In the first chapter I discussed two components of the movement alphabet: movement concepts (adverbs) and motor skills (verbs). In this chapter I will clarify the content areas in each category.

It is important for teachers to fully understand each content area because this is the "right stuff," the curriculum, for children at the elementary level. Teachers should remember that both movement concepts and motor skills can be learned independently or together and that each can become the focus of a lesson or unit. It would be erroneous to focus primarily on movement concepts at the primary level and leave the motor skills to the intermediate level. Most children never completely master the alphabet, and each letter should be revisited throughout pre-K to sixth grade. A middle school teacher complained to me recently that her students had difficulty in line dancing because they could not perform basic movements. This kind of concern is common in school physical education, but using the movement alphabet can minimize these problems.

Movement Concepts

A child who becomes physically educated has learned the necessary skills to move, using concepts of body awareness (what the body does), space awareness (where the body moves), effort (how the body moves), and relationships (with whom or with what the body moves). These terms will become clear after reflection and use. Each of these content areas will be addressed. The movement concepts

- give teachers and children a movement vocabulary that enhances communication and feedback;
- help children understand efficient versus inefficient movement;
- aid the teacher's ability to analyze movement; teachers should become adept at isolating and observing speed, force production, flow, space, directions, levels, pathways, extensions, body parts, and body shapes (e.g., learning to dribble with the hands requires both heavy and light forces applied to the ball, depending upon the situation);
- provide abundant practice opportunities to learn the motor skills;
- aid the teacher in planning lessons and developing content (see Graham, 1992, for a comprehensive understanding of extensions, refinements, and applications); and
- form the basis for learning educational dance (Purcell, 1994).

Motor Skills

A child who becomes physically educated has learned to perform motor skills that include locomotor patterns (traveling) and manipulative patterns (using hands and feet). As children see and feel their motor skills improving, a great sense of accomplishment—and sometimes relief—can be observed on their faces. Learning the motor skills produces the kind of excitement we experience reading our first challenging book, writing a thoughtful letter, or manipulating a set of figures to solve a problem.

Unfortunately, most children do not learn to perform all the motor skills, and few children comprehend the importance of these skills. Many specialists who know the biomechanics of motor skills fail to teach them, assuming that children already have acquired these skills or that the movement alphabet lacks usefulness in the day-to-day teaching of physical education.

In later sections I will briefly describe and illustrate each locomotor and manipulative motor skill pattern. Four learnable pieces will accompany each motor skill (many more could be included) to help you visualize the parts of the skill that are essential for a mature movement pattern. These learnable pieces, or critical components (Graham, 1992), provide teachers and children with realistic, observable, and assessable motor skill outcomes. For example, learning how to perform a mature leaping pattern may take children years to accomplish. However, learning to leap using the arms to create momentum (a learnable piece) can be accomplished much more quickly. Often it is better to work on parts of the motor skill, instead of the whole movement, during the initial learning stages. The learnable pieces can be the focus of a lesson or a series of lessons. A more complete treatment of the motor skills can be found elsewhere (Gallahue, 1989; Graham et al., 1993; Thomas et al., 1988; Wickstrom, 1977).

Body Awareness

Children enter school with little awareness or understanding of what the body does while moving. In fact, many adults have difficulty acquiring new skills because they too lack body awareness that they could have learned during their formative years. When children develop body awareness they can demonstrate numerous ways to move individual parts (keeping others inactive, sometimes in unison, other times in opposition). Body awareness involves being able to identify body parts, balance from different bases of support, and create body shapes and positions in a limited area. This category includes nonlocomotor movements, such as bending, stretching, twisting, and turning. Table 3.1 outlines the content and gives descriptors or cues for each movement concept in the body awareness category.

Table 3.1 Movement Concepts for Body Awareness

Content areas	Descriptors/cues
Body parts	Head, shoulders, torso, arms, legs, toes, and others
Shapes	
Curved	Round like a tire
Twisted	Part of the body remains still while another part turns away from it, like a pretzel
Narrow	Arms and legs are close together and look thin
Wide	Arms and legs are stretched out
Symmetrical	If you cut your body in two, both sides would be the same
Asymmetrical	If you cut your body in two, both sides would look different
Base of support	Balance and support of the body's weight
Nonlocomotor	
Swing	Big, free, rhythmic movements of the body part(s)
Sway	A controlled swing using smaller movements, side to side or front to back
Twist	See above
Turn	Circular movement of the body or parts; quarter-, half-, three-quarter, 360 degrees or full
Bend/curl	Flexing, closing the body up, bringing body parts together
Stretch	Extending your arms and legs away from torso
Sink	Gradually moving downward
Push	Moving an object away from you
Pull	Drawing an object toward you
Shake	Shivering; you feel an earthquake

Space Awareness

When children play youth soccer often 10 or more players are trying to kick the ball at the same time: Children do not understand just where the body can move to dribble, pass, head, and kick. To dodge an object safely and successfully children must be cognizant of available space. All movement takes place in space. Movements can be attempted in or at various directions, levels, and pathways. Extensions involve moving the arms and legs various distances away from the body in general or self-space. Catching a ball can require either near or distant arm extension, depending on the situation. Table 3.2 outlines the content and gives descriptors or cues for each movement concept in the space awareness category.

Table 3.2   Movement Concepts for Space Awareness

Content areas	Descriptors/cues
General space	The empty or open space other than one's personal space
Self-space	The space in the immediate area where you don't touch anyone or anything
Directions	
Forward	The front of your body leads
Backward	The back of your body leads
Sideways	Your right or left side leads
Up	Your body goes toward the sky
Down	Your body goes toward the ground
Levels	
Low	Below the waist
Middle	Between the shoulders and waist
High	Above the shoulders
Pathways	
Curved	Bent line
Straight	Same direction, no curve or bend
Zigzag	Straight lines with sharp turns
Extensions	
Near	Arms and legs move a little from the body
Far	Arms and legs move away from body

Effort Concepts

Watch a class of children running or jogging. Some move effortlessly and are smooth and coordinated, while others move rigidly and heavily and are uncoordinated. Running efficiency has less to do with using proper mechanics than with improving the quality of the movement. Effort concepts describe how the body moves to vary its speed, force, and flow. Children need plenty of practice in a variety of contexts to tense and relax muscles efficiently. This ability is the basis for the speed, force, and flow of a particular movement. Table 3.3 depicts the content and gives descriptors or cues for each movement in the category of effort concepts.

Table 3.3   Movement Concepts for Effort

Content areas	Descriptors/cues
Speed	
Fast	Quick; sudden; explosive; anaerobic; muscles tight
Slow	Careful; drawn out; sustained; aerobic; muscles relaxed
Force	
Strong	Strong; intense; heavy; muscles tight or tense
Light	Easy; weak; buoyant; slight; muscles loosened up
Flow	
Bound	Controlled; jerky; robotic; restricted; muscles tight
Free	Smooth; fluid; continuous; muscles move easily

Relationship Concepts

Many children learn by watching skilled performers. They may notice the position of the arms and legs to the bat or how partners work together to block a volleyball sailing over the net. Movement often involves groups, a partner, and objects (striking implements, balls, hoops, mats, lines on the floor). Children should understand the relationship of their bodies to these objects and people. Advanced sports, games, dance, and exercise are extremely difficult for someone who underestimates the dynamic relationships inherent in these activities. Table 3.4 outlines the content and gives examples of cues for each relationship concept.

Locomotor Patterns

Children learn immature forms of walking, running, jumping, and even dodging before they

Table 3.4 Movement Concepts for Relationships

Content areas	Examples of cues
Objects or others	
Between/ inside/outside	Find a way to move inside the hoop.
Around/through	Circle around your partner to catch the ball.
In front of/ behind/beside	Place your body beside the target.
Under/over	Move your body under the rope.
On/off	Jump on the box and roll off.
Across	Travel across the mat; you choose the way.
Above/below	Strike the balloon above your head; now hit it below your knees.
Partners	
Leading	Run ahead of and lead your partner.
Following	Slide behind and follow your partner.
Meeting	Move toward the net when striking.
Parting	Move away from your partner.
Matching	Skip in unison, side-by-side to match your partner.
Mirroring	Perform opposite movements with your partner, like being a mirror.

enter school. If you ask a child "Are you a good runner?" you will probably be answered with a resounding yes. In fact, some children, overestimating their ability, attempt to race older children and adults. They are often surprised to find the race was a mismatch. Most children demonstrate immature and inefficient locomotor patterns during the primary years. By providing appropriate opportunities for practice, feedback, and reinforcement teachers can foster improvement. At the university level, I typically allot 3 hours of class time to help teachers learn about the locomotor skills. Each semester a handful comment, "I can't believe I didn't know this before; I wish I had known this 10 years ago!"

Walking

Watch children walking down the school halls. Nearly all children can get from point A to point B, but do they display efficient and mature form? Are they fluid and relaxed? Walking is a lifetime skill. It has received greater attention in recent years because of the risks attributed to running and jogging. Walking is simply placing one foot in front of the other (weight transfer) while keeping one foot in contact with the ground at all times (see Figure 3.3). The heel of the foot contacts the ground first and transfers the body's weight to the middle and then the ball of the foot.

Learnable pieces

- Walk so that your arms swing in opposition to the legs.
- Walk, keeping your feet pointed straight ahead, in straight lines.
- Walk lightly and relaxed, not jerkily.
- Walk with the head erect and shoulders straight.

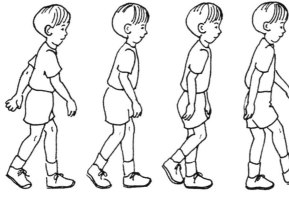

Figure 3.3 Mature walking pattern.

Running and Jogging

Children value running fast. Status is ascribed to the child who is fastest in the class, grade level, or school. More important, running is probably the most essential locomotor skill to become an efficient mover in a variety of activities. It is commonly used in combination with almost every other locomotor and manipulative pattern. Developing a mature running pattern is analogous to learning addition in math: One can't perform other functions well before mastering this basic skill. Running efficiently follows the same principle as walking, with the addition of a period of suspension (both feet off the ground), greater forward body lean, and higher knee bend. There are two choices when placing the feet on the ground (see Figure 3.4). Jogging involves the same foot placement as the walk (heel, mid-foot, ball of the foot). Sprinting, however, involves performing the run on the balls of the feet for short distances (less than 200 yards). Children may need help choosing the correct technique for various activities.

Learnable pieces

- Run with arm and leg opposition.
- Run with relaxed arms and upper body.
- Sprint, staying up on the balls of the feet.
- Jog, placing the foot in this sequence: heel, mid-foot, ball of foot.

Jumping and Landing

Toddlers initially attempt jumping—without a plan for landing—when they bounce off couches, beds, chairs, and other furniture. Nevertheless, an efficient jump and landing can be a complex movement for many children. Although often misunderstood, it is probably the second most widely used locomotor pattern. Jumping will increase height and distance and can be rhythmic

Figure 3.4   Mature running pattern.

Figure 3.5   Mature jumping pattern.

movement, as in jumping rope. Moreover, jumping frequently is combined with catching, punting, and volleying; sometimes it is used with throwing and striking.

Jumping can take three forms: (a) taking off with two feet and landing on two feet (see Figure 3.5); (b) taking off with one foot and landing on two feet; and (c) taking off with two feet and landing on one foot. Children should practice each form extensively. Creating momentum with the arms, bending the knees, and landing on the ball of the foot or feet are essential to an efficient jump. Jumps for height and distance are normally prepared with a short run. When children are ready, blend hopping, sliding, dodging, and leaping with jumping.

Learnable pieces

- Jump, taking off from the ball of the foot or feet; land either the same or a different way.
- Jump and land using your arms (swinging up and forward).
- Jump, practicing buoyant landings.
- Jump, using variations in knee bends.

Sliding

Children often think sliding is diving on the ground feet first, a potentially dangerous action they use primarily in baseball, football, soccer, and other competitive sports and games. I want children to understand that sliding is a step and run combination used to change direction quickly. Seen in this manner it takes on a more important function. Sliding is the fourth most often used locomotor skill in physical education. It can combine readily with galloping, leaping, jumping, and each manipulative skill. Most team and individual sports and dances will require a mature sliding pattern. An efficient slide moves from side to side, and the same foot always leads the movement (see Figure 3.6).

Learnable pieces

- Slide, staying on the balls of the feet.
- Practice arm and leg extensions, near and far, when sliding.
- Slide, bending the knees.
- Use the arms to gain speed while sliding.

Galloping

When I hear the term gallop, I envision nursery school children prancing like horses. This movement fantasy for young children, if mastered, transfers easily to games and sports. Fencing uses this motor skill extensively. Galloping provides a crafty change of direction when needed and is easily combined with the run, leap, and jump. It follows the same principles as sliding, but in a forward or backward direction: One foot leads and the other follows, without crossing (see Figure 3.7). A forward step and close (slide) pattern uses the same foot leading the movement. It is important for children to lead this movement with the nondominant foot, once the dominant side has been practiced.

Figure 3.6   Mature sliding pattern.

Figure 3.7   Mature galloping pattern.

Learnable pieces

- Practice galloping by leading with the right foot, then the left.
- Practice bending the knees to absorb the force when moving quickly.
- Gallop, staying on the balls of the feet.
- Gallop with a smooth, rhythmic motion.

Leaping

Leaping is a misunderstood locomotor pattern. Think of ballerinas leaping across the stage, wide receivers leaping to catch a ball in the end zone, and high hurdlers leaping over a series of barriers in the Olympics. Children often confuse the leap with a jump or hop, yet it has a utility all its own. Leaping is an exaggerated run, weight transferred from one foot to the other, but with a period of suspension. Leaping and running are a common combination; another grouping to try is sliding, galloping, and leaping. An efficient leap lifts the body vertically: It uses knee bend, vigorous swinging of the arms, and landing on the ball of the foot (see Figure 3.8).

Learnable pieces

- Try leaping and stretching, the legs wide while airborne.
- Use the arms to create momentum.
- Bend the knees to create a takeoff and longer flight.
- Practice landing on the ball of the right foot; then on the left foot.

Hopping

Rabbits don't hop! Teachers often ask children to hop like bunnies. Hopping is taking off with one foot and landing on the same foot (ball of the foot) (see Figure 3.9). I have yet to see a rabbit do this. Hopping is a dynamic (moving) balance on one limb. Children will have trouble hopping if they cannot balance on one foot. The knee of the inactive leg should be bent behind the body. With the knees flexed, the arms aid in gaining height, distance, and balance. Hopping is tiring because much of the body's weight lifts and lands on the same leg.

Learnable pieces

- Practice hopping with the left and right side of the body; alternate the right and left foot in a rhythmic manner.

Figure 3.8   Mature leaping pattern.

Figure 3.9 Mature hopping pattern.

- Stay on the ball of the foot to take off and land.
- Use the arms to create momentum.
- Bend the knees and flex the ankles when hopping.

Skipping

Kareem Abdul-Jabbar would skip backward during NBA contests while waiting for the opponents to move down the floor. I believe he did this as a transition, instead of a walk or run. Skipping is like the sidestroke in swimming: It is not competitive but keeps one moving without resorting to a vigorous movement. Actually, skipping is an excellent motor skill to help children to learn about lateralization. Skipping is a combination of a step and hop using one side of the body, then shifting the process to the other side of the body (see Figure 3.10). Children commonly have difficulty learning to skip at the primary level, but following another child who demonstrates a mature pattern can help them learn.

Learnable pieces

- Practice skipping with arms in opposition to legs.
- Practice skipping, staying up on the balls of the feet.
- Practice skipping with a relaxed upper body and arms.
- Practice skipping to a beat.

Chasing, Fleeing, Dodging, and Faking

These motor skills are combinations of the previous eight locomotor patterns. During dynamic games it is up to a child to determine which locomotor patterns, in combination with nonloco-

Figure 3.10 Mature skipping pattern.

motor patterns, are best for chasing, fleeing, dodging, and faking. Trying to overtake a person or object is chasing; trying to avoid a person or object is fleeing; trying to change direction (avoiding the original line of movement) is dodging; deceiving a person by moving the eyes, head, shoulders, or other body parts is faking (see Figure 3.11). These motor skills should be practiced individually and then in combination. Mature chasing, fleeing, dodging, and faking are true tests of a child's ability to master the locomotor patterns. These motor skills have been addressed in greater detail by Belka (1994).

Learnable pieces

- Practice quick pathway and directional changes while traveling.
- Practice watching your partner's waist while traveling to catch him or her.
- Practice changing speeds while fleeing from a partner.
- Practice faking your partner by quick movements while traveling.

Manipulative Patterns

I've always enjoyed crunching numbers, reading biographies, and finding information for friends, but none of these activities compares to my favorite motor skills, throwing and catching a ball. Manipulating an object with the feet or hands is one of the most challenging tasks a person can learn. Recently I observed four college students playing Hacky Sack (footbag juggling). It was fascinating because of their skill and excellent manipulative abilities. Most children who try

juggling with the feet have great difficulty in keeping the footbag consistently in the air. Children, however, can accomplish the same task successfully with balloons.

Children love to manipulate objects. Manipulative motor skills can be self-propelling activities (no pun intended) if taught in the right way. I wonder how many times Nolan Ryan, former pitcher for the Texas Rangers, has thrown a ball? Why do children and adults perform any manipulative pattern thousands of times? Think how much mastery of throwing, catching, striking, volleying, dribbling, and kicking can increase activity options throughout life.

Throwing

Throwing and catching are the meat and potatoes of the manipulative diet. The child who becomes proficient in throwing and catching will probably find that learning to strike, dribble with the hands, and volley come naturally. I often discover that children resist activities requiring these motor skills because they lack proficiency, understanding, and perhaps courage. The fundamental rule for throwing is to use movement in the whole body, not just the shoulder, arm, and hand. The combinations of run and throw, jump and throw, leap and throw, and slide and throw will challenge children at higher levels of proficiency.

Throwing is done in three basic ways: underhand, overhand, and sidearm. Teach the underhand first. An underhand throw works best when children face the target. The overhand and sidearm patterns require turning the side of the body (left if the child is right-handed) toward the target. All three patterns benefit from a backswing

Figure 3.11   Mature chasing, fleeing, dodging, and faking patterns.

of the throwing arm. Lead with the elbow, away from the body; transfer the weight from the back foot to the front foot, twisting at the hips; step with the foot opposite the throwing hand; and follow through or extend the arm toward the target (see Figures 3.12, 3.13, and 3.14). It usually is best to synchronize the throwing arm and opposite leg. Begin describing angles of release with children; 45 degrees is best for maximum distances. Some children may be ready to combine a step and sideward hop at the beginning of the throw to create greater force.

Learnable pieces

- Position the body in relation to the target (facing for underhand throw; sideways for overhand and sidearm).

- Practice throwing with leg opposition.
- Practice shifting the body weight from the back foot to the front foot.
- Practice pointing the fingers to the target to encourage the follow-through.

Catching

It always amazes me to watch children catch for the first time. If fear isn't already a factor, it soon will condition a child's catching once he or she has been hit in the face or nose. Many children assume that the object to be caught should come directly to them, instead of them going to the object. Proficient catching requires eye contact, the most violated principle of catching; moving toward the object; catching with the hands, instead of the body;

Figure 3.12   Mature underhand throw.

Figure 3.13   Mature overhand throw.

Figure 3.14   Mature sidearm throw.

bending the arms and relaxing the fingers; and absorbing the force, by giving with the ball or taking a step backward. Adjust the hands depending on the level of the ball, with the pinkies together for a low ball below the waist and the thumbs together for a high ball above the waist (see Figure 3.15). The combinations of catch and throw, catch and kick, catch and strike, catch and dribble, and catch and volley will test children's abilities when they are ready to learn more skills.

Learnable pieces

- Practice moving to the object from all directions (forward, backward, left, right).

- Judge where the ball will land by watching it all the way into the hands.

- Relax the hands and arms upon impact.

- Practice hand positions for high- and low-level catches.

Striking

When my younger brother was 5 years old, I attempted to teach him to strike with a long Fred Flintstone club and ball. He was fairly successful, because I pitched the ball to where he would swing. Any variation in my pitch outside his narrow striking zone, however, would decrease his chances for contact. Striking may be the most difficult manipulative pattern. A baseball player who successfully hits the ball into play every third time at bat is considered a great hitter.

Striking is an extension of catching (eye contact) and throwing (overhand, sidearm, underhand), except that the object is struck with an implement while it is stationary or moving. The striking implements can be short or long (hands, paddles, rackets, bats, sticks, clubs), but they should be appropriate in length and weight for children.

Striking may require a forehand or backhand motion. A proficient striking pattern involves

Figure 3.15   Mature catching.

Figure 3.16 Mature striking pattern.

turning one side of the body to the object in preparation for a backswing; a weight shift from back to front; trunk twist; opposition of the striking arm and leg; and arm extension and a follow-through upon contact. The knees should be bent and the grip solid on the striking implement; contact should be in the center of the striking implement; and the swinging motion should be level or fluid in a vertical or horizontal plane (see Figure 3.16). Most skilled players can swing without consciously thinking of how the body parts move, but children demonstrate great variation in their abilities to sequence the learnable pieces rapidly.

Learnable pieces

- Shift the body weight and turn the hips.
- Use a firm wrist and elbow with short implements.
- Follow through in the direction of the target.
- Turn the side to the object; step to swing.

Volleying

The first attempts at volleying can be observed when a child gets a balloon. It's just more fun to strike a balloon than to hold, squeeze, or throw it. Volleying is a specialized striking skill using an underhand or overhand pattern. The striking can be done with the hand, head, knee, or foot. Attention should be given to volleying with both hands and arms (set and bump). A mature pattern follows the same principles listed earlier for striking. Remind children to bend the knees; make solid enough contact to control the object's direction; keep the wrists stiff; align the body to the object; and follow through (see Figure 3.17).

Learnable pieces

- Practice stepping with the opposite foot and volleying.

Underhand   Overhand

Figure 3.17 Mature volleying.

- Practice moving under the ball.
- Practice pointing the striking body part to the target.
- Practice working the legs by bending the knees throughout the movement.

Dribbling With the Hands

Most children are intrigued and challenged to bounce a ball and see its response to varying amounts of force and direction over long periods of time. Dribbling is continuous bouncing or striking, with two hands or one, in a downward direction. The skill is useful for basketball, speedball, and other educational games teachers and children create. Teachers should emphasize that a mature pattern includes pushing, rather than slapping, the ball; firm, flexible wrists; consistent force and rhythm; waist-high bouncing; good body balance; the body leaning slightly for-ward with the knees bent; and dribbling without looking at the ball (see Figure 3.18).

Learnable pieces

- Use fingerpads of the hand to dribble with control.
- Practice with the head up and eyes looking right and left.
- Practice using a pushing action of the arm and hand.
- Practice keeping the ball away from the feet, yet close to the body.

Kicking, Dribbling With the Feet, and Punting

One of my favorite lessons is teaching children to kick. Children enjoy striking a ball with different parts of the foot; this helps to partially explain

Figure 3.18   Mature dribbling pattern.

Figure 3.19   Mature kicking.

the growth of youth soccer in North America. Kicking and catching are combination skills that benefit all children learning them. The cardinal principle of kicking, like throwing, is whole-body movement, not isolated action in the hip, leg, and foot. A good kick also follows the characteristics of the mature striking pattern. In teaching, emphasize that the hip leads the kicking motion; the support leg is bent and the trunk leans back slightly. Contact should be directed slightly below the center of the ball. Kicking with the inside of the foot is best for short kicks and with the instep (shoelaces), not the toes, for long, powerful kicks (see Figure 3.19). Kicking with the instep requires approaching the ball from the side, keeping the foot down and toe out. Dribbling with the feet (Figure 3.20), including collecting and trapping, and punting (Figure 3.21), the most complicated kick, are variations of the kicking pattern that require understanding and additional practice.

Learnable pieces

- Practice stepping into the kick; take two steps and kick.
- Contact the ball with the instep, shoelaces, or Velcro strips.
- Follow through the kick high, toward the target.
- Keep the eyes on the ball; contact the ball below its center point.

Summary

What content should elementary school children learn in physical education, given that most stu-

Figure 3.20 Mature dribbling with the feet.

Figure 3.21 Mature punting.

dents will receive three or fewer class periods a week with a specialist? What is important for children to know, value, and do? I argue that the alphabet of movement (movement concepts and motor skills) should replace the traditional content of physical education, an outdated curriculum. Although games and sports may satisfy some students and teachers, they meet the developmental needs of very few children aged 5 to 12.

In contrast, a developmental curriculum uses recent research about how children progress through predictable stages of learning. An important aspect of readiness in physical education is that producing physically educated children requires deferring more complex sports. Chil-dren should not be pushed into competitive sports, games, dance, and exercise activities before they are ready. Most children are not ready for these complex activities.

The curriculum should not be an albatross weighing down both teacher and students. Rather, it can be a carefully planned diet to prepare children for a lifetime of healthy play. Without a developmental plan it is too easy for teachers to offer a smorgasbord of activities leaving children malnourished. This chapter has outlined the essential movement concepts and motor skills. The mature form for each motor skill, with learnable pieces, has been offered for those specialists who wish to change elementary physical education for children.

Chapter 4

Principles for Teaching Movement Concepts and Skills

My first formal experience teaching was a 15-minute minilesson during undergraduate training. The task was to teach a group of second graders about personal and general space. My lesson plan included 20 activities to help the children understand the concept. After introducing myself to the children, I challenged each of them, "Find your own space in this area and get ready for activity." I had a solid understanding of the content; the results, however, were disastrous. Ten children scattered beyond the blacktop boundaries, some over 50 yards away, while others kept moving without locating a home. I lost patience with their responses. Once the children were settled where they could see and hear, the lesson dragged along, making 15 minutes seem like 15 hours for the children and me. Over the next several years I struggled not with the content but with my delivery and teaching skills. I had not understood how intricate teaching could be.

Teaching is managing the learning environment to shape and even predict desired changes in student behavior. It is a complex skill that requires knowledge of children and content and thinking through strategies. Teachers must intend to change the behaviors of the children they work with. Chapter 1 outlined 20 essential student outcomes or behavioral changes that define the physically educated person; they are benchmarks of a good physical education program (see Figure 1.2).

In the past two decades scholars have given considerable attention to the science of teaching physical education. They have observed and videotaped, rated, coded, interviewed, and placed physical education classes, students, and teachers under a variety of experimental conditions. As a result, we have a wealth of knowledge about teaching children, although there is much more to learn and many more questions to ask and answer. Silverman (1991), summarizing 20 years of research on teaching motor skills, lists the characteristics effective and experienced physical education teachers have (see Figure 4.1).

Don't overlook the list because you see the term *research*. Research is simply a systematic way to answer important questions about real schools, teachers, and students in physical education classes. These traits of effective teachers might just as well characterize a circus ringmaster, noted artist, symphony conductor, or professional pool player. Graham (1992) translated the results of research on teaching into everyday language for physical education specialists. In Figure 4.2, I outline the pedagogical topics in his book that provide a foundation for improving teaching skills. The theory is solid, and the ideas work in the real world of schools.

Plan for class management and student learning

Anticipate situations and make contingency plans

Plan and monitor for differences in students' motor skills

Require much information to plan

Have a repertoire of teaching styles and know their use

Provide accurate and focused explanations and demonstrations

Provide adequate time for student practice

Maximize appropriate student practice

Minimize inappropriate student practice

Minimize student waiting time

Figure 4.1   Characteristics of effective or experienced teachers.
From "Research on Teaching in Physical Education" by S. Silverman, 1991, *Research Quarterly for Exercise and Sport*, **62**(4), p. 358. Copyright 1991 by AAHPERD. Adapted by permission.

Effective planning
Set induction and getting lessons started
Strategies to minimize off-task behavior
Giving clear instructions, pinpointing, and using visual aids
Motivating children to practice, by using

  – invitation
  – intratask variation
  – task sheets
  – learning centers
  – realistic expectations

Observing and analyzing children's movement patterns
Using extensions, refinements, and applications to develop content
Using feedback strategies
Indirect and direct teaching styles
Building positive feelings in children

Figure 4.2   Graham's (1992) pedagogical topics.

How should you teach the alphabet of movement (concepts and skills)? If you plan a series of lessons on kicking, for example, how can you teach this motor skill most efficiently? What does a mature kick look like? Can you arrange for a visual model to help children comprehend a mature kick? What can a teacher say and do to ensure positive changes in children's kicking? How do the body parts, working alone and together, perform a successful kick? Finally, how should teachers help children learn to kick in a way that will be useful in games, sports, and even dances?

In this chapter I address three objectives. First, I define teaching and describe some research about effective instruction in physical education. Second, I give specific examples of pedagogical principles for teaching selected movement concepts and motor skills. Third, I list counterproductive and inappropriate teaching practices teachers should avoid in movement concept and motor skill lessons. Although we can assume that generic teaching principles apply across all the content areas (movement concepts and motor skills, fitness, dance, gymnastics, and games), the uniqueness of the movement alphabet deserves special treatment.

Principles for Teaching the Movement Alphabet

Introducing the movement concepts and motor skills requires that teachers carefully plan and implement units and lessons to make them meaningful, satisfying, and appropriate for children. Elementary physical education experts (Council on Physical Education for Children,

1992) agree on 26 developmentally appropriate practices for teaching children. Six of these practices have specific implications for teaching the movement alphabet.

- Teachers should give students "frequent and meaningful age-appropriate practice opportunities" to understand the movement concepts and build competence and confidence in the motor skills.
- Teachers should design activities for "both the physical and cognitive development of children." When learning the movement alphabet, children should be "encouraged to question, integrate, analyze, communicate, and apply cognitive concepts."
- The motor skills (especially walking and jogging/running) should be used to develop physical fitness in a "supportive, motivating, and progressive manner."
- All students should be "involved in activities that allow them to remain continuously active."
- All children should be "given the opportunity to practice skills at high rates of success and adjusted for their individual skill levels."
- Sufficient equipment (quantity, size, and weight) should be available to maximize practice opportunities and build confidence in skill acquisition.

It is always prudent to plan experiments for behavioral change and think through the available options. Figure 4.3 provides a checklist to use in planning lessons on the movement alphabet. Just as an airplane pilot needs a flight plan, a teacher should decide where she is going.

Teaching Movement Concepts

Teaching the movement concepts can be scary for instructors who are accustomed to a traditional model. Going to the playground or gymnasium to teach spatial awareness or flow can arouse anxiety. Most children become interested in any movement content when they grasp its relevance and if it is taught well. Movement is one of the primary means for children to learn about the world around them; they already are movement beings.

I find that children enjoy learning movement concepts because the ideas stimulate creative ways to move the body and vary the motor skills. Music and a drum are important aids in teaching the movement concepts. Music not only motivates children but also, more important, helps them become aware of the internal body, giving them a sense of timing and the underlying rhythm and beat for various movements.

Consulting a thesaurus for exciting synonyms for movement tasks is helpful. For example, you might enhance the challenge to "move at a low level (below the knees) without touching others" by saying, "Show me how snakes slither in the grass." The term slither emphasizes the level and speed while adding the imagery of hissing animal sounds. As children are ready, define each movement concept and give its spelling; the words can easily become part of a child's language development. Schmidt (borrowing from Fitts & Posner, 1967) observes that in the verbal-cognitive stage of motor learning

the learner's first problem is verbal and cognitive, in which the dominant questions are about goal identification, performance

---

What movement concept and/or motor skill will I teach today?

How does today's theme coincide with NASPE's outcomes of a "Physically Educated Person" (see chapter 1), the curriculum, the organizing center, and tomorrow's lesson?

What learnable piece will I focus on?

What will I say to give specific and useful feedback to children?

How will I modify tasks to accommodate individual children?

Have I arranged for a visual model(s) of the movement concept or motor skill?

What will I say and do to stress good movement?

How many practice opportunities will there be for each child for each skill?

Will at least 85% of the children be engaged in the concept or skill?

Will I emphasize process or product today?

How will I tie together what the children learn in class today?

Figure 4.3 Prelesson self-checklist for teaching the movement alphabet.

evaluation, what to do (and what not to do), when to do it, how to stand or grasp the apparatus, [and] what to look at. (1991, p. 173)

Body Awareness

When relating the movement concepts to body awareness, consider these principles.

- Learning body shapes (curved, twisted, narrow, wide, symmetrical, asymmetrical) helps children identify and isolate where and how their body parts move. If I show children a picture of Michael Jordan performing a dunk shot, the first questions are What are the body parts doing? and What body shape(s) is he making? They quickly learn to think about body parts and the shape of the body as they attempt various movements. Children can draw themselves (body parts) on butcher block paper—an excellent partner or group activity. Using a jointed action figure, such as a Teenage Mutant Ninja Turtle, adds a fine visual aid to demonstrate how the body parts twist and turn.
- The base of support and balance are essential in every movement. Have the children practice each movement with different bases of support, emphasizing body balance and control. Ask children which base of support works best.
- The nonlocomotor movements (swing, sway, twist, turn, bend, curl, stretch, sink, push, pull, and shake) are important elements in every movement. List, discuss, and apply these concepts in various combinations. For example, stretching and bending the arms are easily taught together.

Space Awareness

The following principles help in teaching children the concepts of spatial awareness.

- Children initially should learn to perform movements in self-space. Subsequent lessons moving between self-space and general space will be especially helpful. Nevertheless, children must demonstrate mastery and control in a confined space before moving in open areas where there are peers and objects to consider.

- Integrate directions and pathways as children are ready. Teachers can draw diagrams of directions and pathways on cards or poster paper to help children visualize and understand the movement concepts. Having children curl into a ball and then uncurl is a good way for them to understand and apply body extensions.
- Most children enjoy working at low levels; the trick is to encourage them to work at high levels. Outdoor play equipment such as bars, beams, and milk crates may attract children to the necessary variety of experiences. Most high-level work requires dynamic balance, jumping, and landing.

Effort Concepts

When relating the movement concepts to effort, consider these principles.

- Quick, sudden, and explosive (fast speed) movements are not necessarily best, contrary to what many children assume. Change and contrast speeds for varied movements. Using a drum, metronome, and music can enhance sustained and deliberate movements.
- Tensing and relaxing muscle groups, such as the arms, legs, and stomach, can convey the concept of force, although it does not always apply in dynamic settings. Use the motor skills of jumping and landing, galloping and skipping, leaping, kicking, throwing, and striking to illustrate moving from a light to strong movement.
- Creative imagery helps children learn the concept of flow, both bound and free. For example, children understand bound movements if we ask them to move like robots or weight lifters. Similarly, to explain free movement have children pretend to fly like eagles. They should practice movements in slow motion, requiring muscle integration and sequencing, and attempt smooth, continuous swinging and swaying movements, as if they are windmills.

Relationship Concepts

The following guidelines may help in teaching relationships to partners or objects.

- Have children practice the concepts of over, under, around, through, between, inside, outside, in front of, behind, beside, on, off, across, above, and below with both manipulative and outdoor play equipment. Design stations so that children can practice a variety of relationship concepts without waiting for turns. Obstacle courses, even with limited resources, will help children comprehend the position of the body in relation to an object or series of objects. For example, a task might be "Find three ways to go through the hoop."

- Working with partners is exciting for children. Leading and following can be the focus of a lesson, using the locomotor patterns as subthemes. Likewise, teach children meeting and parting movements, accompanied by a drum beat or music. Mirroring and matching movements are best accomplished with partners and small groups, depending on age appropriateness. Equipment is often unnecessary, as children can practice skipping side by side. Children enjoy leading and following various movements, and teachers should tap into their creativity.

Teaching Motor Skills

Teaching motor skills is probably easier for most specialists than teaching movement concepts. Understanding how children pass through predictable stages of motor development (see Gallahue, 1989; Graham et al., 1993; Wickstrom, 1977) can help in the planning and teaching of motor skills. Although the goal is to strive for mature motor skill forms as appropriate, teachers should allow for a child's unique style.

Design motor skill tasks to challenge, but not frustrate, children. Moreover, use a wide variety of learning experiences, or tasks, that elicit the same outcome. To teach throwing, it is important to modify this motor skill using each movement concept. Some modifications are more fundamental than others. The teacher must carefully order the learning tasks from simple to complex. Teachers can design a learning wheel with overlapping movement concepts and motor skills (see Graham et al., 1987, and Figure 4.4). The wheel is an excellent tool for teaching children that greatly increases their comprehension of the movement alphabet.

Combining the movement concepts with each motor skill produces a wide variety of learning experiences. The trick in teaching effectively at the elementary level, as most teachers know, is

to transfer previous learning to new concepts, finding creative enough ways to practice the same basic skill so that children remain interested and even intrigued. The video industry produces new games each month to attract children's interest, but the fine hand-eye coordination skill that players use for all of these games is the same. The mental challenges and motor complexity increase as children gain competence and confidence with the controls.

In teaching the motor skills and combinations consider the following 10 guidelines and developmentally appropriate principles.

- Focus on and observe only one part or segment of a movement at a time—the "learnable piece." For example, analyze only the child's foot placement (staying on the balls of the feet) while observing a sprinting pattern. Analyzing the arms (and opposition), body lean, or knee bend can occur in subsequent lessons.
- Analyze the mechanics of movement for each motor skill (Schurr, 1975). For example, for jumping and landing you should observe the

Base of support and balance	Weight even over both feet
Production of force	Hips, knees, and ankles bent
Direction of application of force	Vertical or horizontal
Head, neck, eye focus	Head and eyes upward
Follow-through	Extend body parts
Force absorption	Buoyant landings

- List, discuss, and apply those combinations of motor skills that typically are sequenced, as children are ready for them. For example, running, jumping and landing, catching, and throwing are often used in combination.
- Remember that attempting a motor skill is different from learning it. Acquiring a motor skill involves "an individual's ability to consistently achieve a goal(s) under a wide variety of conditions" (Higgins, 1991, p. 125).
- Encourage children to listen as they move; they should refrain from talking, screaming, and yelling unless the communication is about an important movement strategy with a partner or group.
- Avoid using lines or squads to teach the motor skills. Many teachers have discovered that a mass formation teaches responsibility

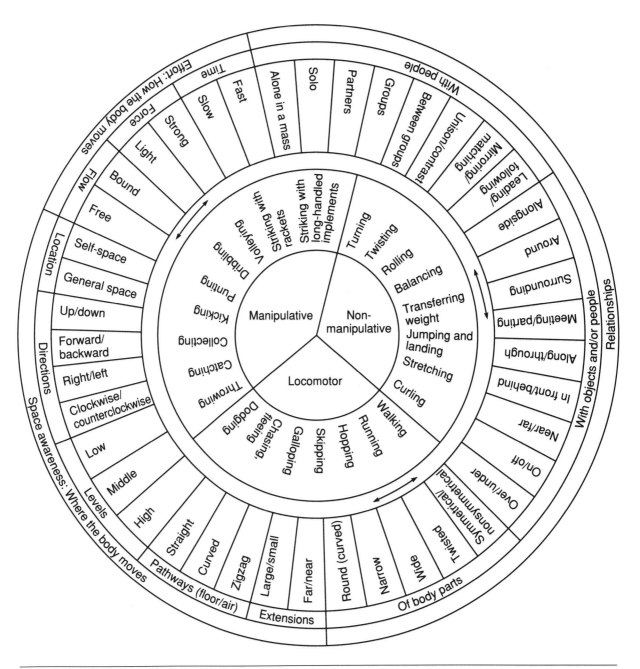

Figure 4.4   Movement analysis wheel of movement concepts and motor skills.
From *Children Moving* (2nd ed.) (p. 32) by G. Graham, S. Holt/Hale, and M. Parker, 1987, Mountain View, CA: Mayfield.
Copyright 1987 by Mayfield. Reprinted by permission.

and provides many more movement options: It teaches children spatial awareness and safety.

- Have children at mature performance levels practice mental imagery before and during a particular movement.
- Encourage partner and small group work for children who are mature enough. Teaching stations or centers are ideal for learning motor skills and they can increase a child's

social and cooperative skills. Give opportunity for the thrill children feel as their motor skills improve.

- Self-competition should take preference over class competition, especially during the early stages of learning. A dribble relay race with the entire class is inappropriate for children who have difficulty bouncing in self-space. Some educators argue that relay races are rarely, if ever, appropriate for children (Schwager, 1992; Williams, 1992).

- Children should experience high rates of success. This does not necessarily mean a child with an immature striking pattern will hit the target every time. It means providing children a reasonable chance of achieving the instructional goal or learnable piece (for example, side to the target when throwing overhand), considering their level of learning. A teacher might direct the children to strike the ball toward the target on the wall (from 15 feet or closer), keeping the wrist firm. The child is successful if he strikes the wall and keeps the wrist firm. Hitting the bull's-eye would be wonderful, but an unreasonable expectation.

Locomotor Skills

Here are 11 principles for teaching children locomotor patterns. See if you can double this list, based upon your experiences with children.

- Emphasize body balance during static and dynamic movements. For hopping, jumping, and leaping children should land on their feet—not on other body parts. Especially at the primary level, many children think it is humorous to fall down after running or jumping. They should know that efficient movers always land on their feet.
- Do not use running and walking as punishments for off-task behavior. Children should not associate punishment with repetitions or lengthy exercise.
- Have children hop forward, instead of upward, which makes it easier to overcome the force of gravity.
- Give lots of practice in synchronizing the arms and legs in the jump, hop, skip, leap, and slide.
- Use two-foot takeoffs as the first phase in teaching jumping and landing. The takeoff generally determines the flight and landing phases.
- Have children master the prerequisite skills for each of the locomotor patterns. For example, the child must be able to balance on one foot in self-space before hopping on one foot in general space.
- Design lessons that do not overly tire children performing one locomotor pattern. An entire lesson on hopping will fatigue both legs.

- Run with the class as it jogs: This can control pacing and motivate students. Also, have children work with partners who are in similar condition.
- Help children become good runners in a variety of movement forms. Running is not only a track event but also part of many other activities. The forward stride position is preferable to the bunch start because it allows greater versatility.
- When they are ready, have children practice from both sides of the body for leaping, hopping, and galloping.
- Encourage children to practice changes in speed, directions, pathways, levels, and extensions to improve their chasing, fleeing, dodging, and faking. Moreover, children should practice twisting and turning movements as they learn to dodge an object or person. Remind children that the head leads, and the body follows.

Manipulative Skills

Here are 11 strategies that are useful in designing manipulative experiences for children. See if the children can describe the ways you helped them to become better at throwing, kicking, striking, dribbling, or catching.

- Use light, colorful, and soft equipment for children who are at the initial catching stage. Later, give children different sizes and shapes of manipulative equipment to use. Small objects are best for throwing, and larger objects, within reason, are best for catching. Styrofoam art balls are excellent items to check the proficiency level in catching because the wind easily alters the ball's path. Catching the ball requires concentration, moving to the ball, and proper hand position.
- Locate wall space for throwing, catching, kicking, volleying, and striking. The wall often is the best partner. Hula hoop stands and the wall become fine targets for manipulative practice trials.
- Have children demonstrate manipulative movements without equipment. Repetitive *motion practice* is especially helpful for learning to throw, catch, strike, volley, kick, and punt. Teachers should remember that the process (developing a consistent pattern) and not the product (where the object goes) is the key to preparing children for dynamic

movements. Two examples may be instructive: "Class, please show me how you place the hands to catch a ball at a high level." "Children, try twisting and turning the trunk, keeping the feet in place. See how the body coils to gain force and help the bat strike."

- Try to have a beanbag or ball for each child: at a minimum, one ball for every two children.
- Receiving an object from a partner is easier at the initial stages than tossing to oneself. Try to group good throwers with poor catchers. Remember, this curriculum is less concerned about passing a football than learning to project many different types of objects using the overhand, underhand, and sidearm patterns.
- Encourage a free, swinging movement for striking activities. This motor skill requires that children understand the concept of easy flow.
- Have children practice throwing, dribbling, kicking, striking, and catching using the nondominant side after they achieve proficiency with the dominant one.
- Find practical ways to help children strengthen the arm and leg muscles.
- Plastic milk jugs and deflated balls are excellent for learning kicking and punting. Teachers should always seek ways to minimize relocation time.
- When dribbling with the feet, have children skip while simultaneously pushing the ball with alternate feet. This principle will help them run and dribble.
- When dribbling with the hands, children should practice varying the force and level. Dribbling in a figure-8 pathway around traffic cones and dribbling combined with passing are difficult for most children at the elementary level. It helps for most children to master each individual skill before attempting combinations.

Summary

In the first chapter I introduced you to my boyhood friend, Tish, who wanted to improve his kicking skills. As a 9-year-old I helped Tish in a small way by sharing my limited knowledge. Children who have the correct motor skill information and can formulate good analyses can help their peers learn. It is miseducation, however, when children are the primary teachers of any subject matter, especially physical education. Furthermore, it is miseducation (Graham, 1987; Schwager, 1992; Williams, 1992; Wilson, 1976) to assume that games and relays will help children to become competent movers.

Teaching is a complex skill with its own stages of development. To be an effective instructor you will have to acquire and practice a host of teaching behaviors to effect learning and confidence in students. A variety of teaching principles will effectively help children learn the movement alphabet. For children to learn the movement concepts and motor skills, teachers need to know the content and have pedagogical skills. This chapter offers teachers broad principles and developmentally appropriate strategies for teaching the movement alphabet.

Chapter 5

Assessing Children's Progress in Movement Concepts and Skills

We live in an information society. Collecting, analyzing, storing, and retrieving important data is a central part of contemporary life. The trick is to separate the important information from the trivia. If we believe that children's physical education is important, then we should document their learning. More important, the collected data should be longitudinal, objective, and practical.

It's clear to me that most physical educators have not embraced the information society; they do not vigilantly observe children's movement patterns. Nor do they collect data on motor skill acquisition, cognitive understanding, and participation values (Hensley, Lambert, Baumgartner, & Stillwell, 1987; Imwold, Rider, & Johnson, 1982; Veal, 1988). This myopia contributes to keeping assessment a mystery in elementary physical education (Buschner, 1992). Unfortunately, many teachers use participation (showing up) and their subjective feelings or intuition about a child's effort as the sole criteria for assessment. Perhaps the purpose of assessment, for these teachers, is to satisfy the school system's policy of grading children. This narrow view of assessment needs change.

When I finished the sixth grade and headed for junior high, I wondered if Mr. Lewis, the seventh grade physical education teacher, was aware of my ability to move. I wondered if Mr. Wheeler, my elementary teacher, had forwarded any information about my skill and interest in physical education. I was certain that my academic files (report cards, behavior reports, teacher notes, and standardized test scores) followed me to the secondary level. Such data was continually collected and shared to help me understand my learning progress. I was not sure that the physical education department at my school collected, analyzed, shared, and stored data on any child (other than a physical fitness score and a grade).

In many parts of the United States assessment of the movement alphabet is an afterthought. Subjective grades, without supporting data, and physical fitness scores tend to be the rule in today's physical education classes. I believe that too many teachers are content with subjectively grading attitude and effort.

My son's fifth grade report card lists S (satisfactory) or U (unsatisfactory) for physical education; but an S or U is meaningless. What does this grade letter tell me about my son's motor skill, fitness, and affective or cognitive learning? More important, teachers and parents rarely receive an ongoing assessment or formative data about how children are progressing in physical education. Even the children often are left in the dark about their physical education abilities. It is no wonder that many children think they move better than they do. Traditional assessment techniques (norm-referenced tests, subjective impressions, and grades) do not address learning from a developmental perspective (Paris, Lawton, Turner, & Roth, 1991). This chapter focuses on assessing children's progress in learning the movement concepts and motor skills, describing why and how to collect frequent and multidimensional data about psychomotor, cognitive, and affective development.

Why Teachers Often Overlook Assessment

There are many reasons why teachers overlook assessment. Most teachers have not learned how to save enough curricular time for assessing hundreds of children (Graham, 1992). If children receive only 60 minutes a week of physical education, they lack adequate time for instruction, let alone time for assessment. For the program and teacher to survive even at a minimal level, choices must be made about when, how, and what to assess. Just as teachers may not be able to teach all of the movement alphabet, they may be able to document only a sample of the child's learning.

Apparently many other teachers neglect assessment because they have convinced themselves that what they do doesn't matter in the large scheme of things. Children matter, however, and physical education is an integral part of a child's life. To persuade children, parents, and administrators to care about physical education, teachers must believe that what they do will make a difference in the lives of children.

Teachers who use the 20-fun-games-and-sports curriculum may believe not only that assessment takes time away from mirth, but also that attention to learning goals takes too much energy, hard work, and even paper-pushing. For these teachers the physical, mental, and organizational costs are perhaps too great. Teachers who sidestep assessment should consider, however, that all effective teaching includes assessment.

Rationale for Assessment

There are several reasons to make systematic assessments. First, a good program documents the developmental changes that occur in students. These data assist the teacher in checking the curriculum's validity and give students and parents feedback. Second, taking the time to evaluate students tells teachers how well they are teaching the content. Third, collecting the data demonstrates to the school's administration and other teachers that physical education is important for children. It is difficult to defend programs, in times of stiff competition for funds, using only subjective impressions. Objective data on learning is probably the best defense in a field that historically has struggled for respect and support. Fourth, assessment, formal and informal, motivates most children. Most children are excited about the opportunity to perform, providing they have mastered the skill. They want to show everyone what they can do; they want recognition (Stipek & MacIver, 1989).

As teachers, our job is to ensure that children have mastered parts or whole skills before we place them in dynamic settings where failure is apparent to peers. We do children a disservice by not assessing them. Doyle (1980) argues that there is no task to be learned if teachers suspend accountability or assessment. This means that learning and assessment go hand in hand. For example, if we teach children a striking skill it is necessary for the teacher to assess the child's ability to perform that task. Otherwise, why teach the task?

Children want to know from "the expert," the teacher, how they are doing. Often I hear "Watch me, Mr. Buschner." "Is this jump OK?" "I want to show you my stretched shape." One motivation behind a child's request for observation is a desire for teacher approval; I think another motivation is that children want feedback because they want to improve. Effective teachers devote time to assessing a child's reading, math, and language skills on a longitudinal basis. The same should be true in physical education. McGee (1984) reminds us that children feel less threatened if evaluation is at their own level of development. This means teachers showing less concern with intra- and interclass comparisons and more concern with observable changes over time in motor performance.

Paris et al. (1991) offer these suggestions for making assessments from a developmental view.

1. *Assessment should be collaborative and authentic to promote learning and motivation.* Effective assessment "minimizes competition with peers." It invites

teachers and students to share criteria, outcomes, and judgments. Children should be encouraged to set personal mastery goals, instead of performance or competitive goals. Students become more motivated to take tests and perform well if they collaborate with teachers in assessment.

2. *Assessment should be longitudinal.* Student progress should be charted from year to year to demonstrate improvement to students, parents, and teachers. One-shot assessment is inappropriate for measuring personal progress, that is, student strengths and weaknesses.

3. *Assessment should be multidimensional.* Because of the interactive nature of learning, motivation, and achievement, assessment should be multidimensional. Tests should measure what students know, the students' perceptions of their abilities, efficacy, interest, and efforts to achieve goals. Learning processes are just as important as learning products. (p. 18)

I have defined teaching as managing the learning environment to shape and even predict desired changes in *student behavior* (see chapter 4). In documenting desired changes and learning, teachers face many questions. Are children achieving the purposes of elementary physical education? Are they achieving the outcomes of the physically educated person? Are children able to meet the benchmarks established by NASPE? Are they acquiring the movement alphabet (see Figure 5.1)? At a more practical level the questions might include these: How well can this child throw a ball? Is the pattern mature? Does he understand the use of force in movement? Can she modify a run using various path-ways? Do the children cooperate when dribbling, throwing, and catching with a partner? Each area of inquiry can provide a fertile starting point for assessment.

The issue is not whether assessment should occur, but rather how it will occur and how the data will be used to produce competent, confident movers. To determine if students are achieving, teachers must collect data on *each class and child.* This chapter concerns why and how the specialist teacher should document that children are learning the movement alphabet. We will visit the three domains of learning—psychomotor, cognitive, affective—focusing on qualitative and formative assessment. This chapter offers a menu for assessing the movement alphabet; teachers should carefully select those strategies most likely to help children become physically educated.

Although how a child learns depends to some degree on the effectiveness of the teacher and program, these areas, along with grading students, require attention to issues of curriculum and instruction beyond the scope of this book on the movement alphabet (see Graham, 1992; Graham et al., 1993; Jewett & Bain, 1985; McGee, 1984; Safrit, 1990).

Psychomotor Assessment

I no longer advocate that teachers use skill tests or rating scales, unless they have ample resources and time. I will offer five alternatives. I have found that one practical way to assess a child's performance is to use the learnable pieces and descriptors/cues outlined in chapter 3 for each of the movement concepts and motor skills. These terms are also referred to as *critical* or *qualitative* components by Graham (1992). For

---

Are children achieving the five purposes of elementary physical education?

    Developmentally appropriate programs help children:

- Become aware of their movement potential
- Move competently and confidently
- Understand and apply the alphabet of movement
- Become versatile movers
- Value healthy play

Are children achieving the 20 outcomes that define the "Physically Educated Person"?
Are children able to meet NASPE benchmarks for Grades K, 2, 4, and 6?
Are children mastering the movement alphabet?

- Movement concepts
- Motor skills

Figure 5.1   Documenting desired student changes in the movement alphabet.

example, a unit of instruction for third graders might include jumping and landing using strong and light force. A teacher-prepared checklist might include children's names and the critical components in a particular class.

For example, the critical components for jumping and landing (see Figure 5.2) might include takeoff (balls of feet); knee bend (takeoff and landing); arm swing (strong); and buoyant landing (balls of feet and light force). The learnable piece for one or more lessons might be taking off from the balls of the feet. Lesson extensions might include height, distance, over, on, time, forward, backward, force, and various shapes. I can visualize children jumping and landing using hula hoops, jump ropes, benches, balls, and other equipment. The teacher would circulate to observe the children, making a note or a check beside each child's name and the learnable piece. Future lessons would require observations using the remainder of the learnable pieces.

It is helpful to your observations to keep in mind the mature execution of the skill. The idea is to observe analytically so you can share specific and congruent feedback with children immediately or afterward. Ask yourself questions like these: Is this child using the learnable piece appropriately? Can I assume, after watching several trials, that this child has learned this component part of the skill I'm observing? If I vary the task will this child transfer this learnable piece? This microscopic analysis is the level of assessment that you must provide to help children progress toward mastering a skill such as jumping and landing.

A second strategy for documenting a child's ability to perform the movement alphabet is to use task progressions. An easy way to record formative learning is to make notes on a sample of children (try three to start with) on each task. As you keep your back to the wall and circulate to observe, you carry a checksheet including student names and each task, leaving space for your checks or notes (see Figure 5.3).

A third technique for assessing children's motor skills is a variation of the Ratliffe System (Graham et al., 1987). The names of children and their observed developmental levels for various motor skills are recorded and dated (see Figure 5.4). This approach requires the teacher to make informed judgments, on the basis of multiple observations, of the stages of motor skill acquisition. I would suggest categorizing children's abilities into one of three levels, or stages: B for beginning, T for transitional, and M for mature. Teachers should establish clear criteria so that their observations are objective. With effective instructions, many children will demonstrate mature levels in most motor skills by the time they leave elementary school. This kind of data should be passed along to teachers at the secondary level.

A fourth approach for assessing children is to have them use self-evaluations and partner evaluations. Children can be capable data collectors if they know what to observe. Although it takes time for teachers to explain to children the benefits, the drawbacks, and the techniques of self- and partner evaluation, these approaches save teachers time in the long run and can serve as progress reports to parents (Holt/Hale, 1993).

There are two wonderful advantages of self- and partner evaluations. First, children begin to really understand a skill by beginning to analyze its components. Second, the data collected allows

| Date | 5/5 | Class | Mr. Wheeler | | Grade | 5th |

Directions: Observe each child jumping and landing at least five times. Check the learnable piece(s) used by the child in attempting a mature pattern. C = consistently demonstrates this learnable piece; O = occasionally uses this learnable piece; N = never uses this learnable piece.

Names of children	Trials	Takeoff (ball)	Knees (bend)	Arms (strong)	Land (buoyant)	Land (ball)
1. Traci	ᵀᴴᴴᴸ	C	C	C	O	O
2. Bryan	ᵀᴴᴴᴸ I I	C	O	C	N	N
3. Jeff	ᵀᴴᴴᴸ	N	N	O	N	N
4. Brett	ᵀᴴᴴᴸ I I I	C	C	C	C	C
5. Crystal	ᵀᴴᴴᴸ I	O	O	O	N	O

Figure 5.2 Jumping and landing checklist.

Date _____ 10/6 _____ Class _____ Mrs. Watson _____ Grade _____ 3rd _____

Directions: Observe selected children during a lesson. After each task the teacher observes three children's responses to the task. S = successfully completed the task; U = unsuccessfully attempted the task; N = needs assistance.

Task progression	Child		
	Jane	Pete	Carol
1. Dribble and walk, jog, run forward	S	S	S
2. Dribble, changing speeds	S	U	S
3. Slide left and dribble with right hand	U	S	S
4. Slide right and dribble with left hand	U	U	S
5. Slide, changing directions and hands	S	S	S
6. Dribble backward	U	U	U
7. Dribble, using finger pads	S	S	S
8. Dribble tag	S	U	S

Figure 5.3 Task progression for dribbling with the hands for grades 3–4.

Date _____ 4/14 _____ Class _____ Mr. Duffy _____ Grade _____ 4th _____

Directions: Observe each child performing an appropriate task that emphasizes a motor skill(s). This record can be compared from year to year. The teacher should establish criteria for assessing the child's level of learning. For example: B = beginning level (initial attempts at the motor skill that result in an inconsistent pattern or learning product); T = transitional (the child is beginning to control his/her body and/or the object; however, the child expends great energy thinking through and performing the movement); M = mature pattern (a good quality movement that can be applied in a variety of situations; the movement appears fluid and the child accomplishes the motor skill with minimal effort).

Names of children	Motor skills		
	Kicking 9/1/93	Striking 11/9/93	Running 12/6/93
Fred	B	T	T
Sally	T	T	M
Samuel	M	T	M
Natalie	B	B	B
Matilda	T	B	T

Figure 5.4 Developmental checklist.

comparisons between teacher and child observations. As I mentioned in chapter 1, many children believe they have mastered a motor skill if they can perform it at any level. We need to reinforce all children at their current stages of development, but we also need to remind them that there is so much more to learn. It is always helpful to read each part of the assessment form to students and provide them with examples. This is an excellent time to review the critical components (see Figures 5.5 and 5.6).

Finally, remember the value of videotaping the children in your classes (Graham, 1992). Parent aides can easily operate a camcorder, focusing on several children who are learning a motor skill, while the teacher leads the lesson. I would suggest that each child purchase a 120-minute tape to use throughout the elementary years. Good tapes, purchased in bulk, cost about $3 each. If necessary, children can share tapes. If we recorded a child's overhand throwing pattern 5 times during each grade level, just think how

Directions: The children receive a copy of this assessment form, and the teacher reads these directions to them: "Today you will be evaluating your ability to throw. We just finished practicing this motor skill in our lesson called *Spring Training.* Think about all of the throws you made and how well you can throw a ball. How do you feel about your ability when you use your whole body to throw? [Read other tasks to the children.] You have three choices. You may feel you need more practice. You may feel you are getting better. Or you may feel you are good at throwing, for your grade level. Please draw a baseball in the category that represents your feeling. Please write your name, grade, and today's date at the top of the page and take 3 minutes to think about your throwing ability. Be honest and take this assessment seriously. I do."

Student name _____*Eric*_____　Date ____*9/15*____　Grade ____*3rd*____

Tasks	Student self-assessment		
	I need more practice to be okay.	I am getting better.	I am good for my grade.
When I use my whole body to throw . . .		◯	
When I step with my opposite foot . . .			◯
When I throw from a distance . . .		◯	
When I throw to the target (baseball glove) . . .		◯	

Other notes about how well I throw: _____

_____

_____

Figure 5.5　Student self-assessment using the Spring Training learning experience for grades 2–3 (see chapter 9).

easily parents, teachers, and children could see development over time.

Cognitive Assessment

Skillful movement requires thinking. Teachers need to encourage children to think critically about the movement alphabet. The movement concepts and motor skills provide an excellent opportunity for learning vocabulary, numbers, statistics, elementary principles of biomechanics, strategies, and about the many relationships between movement and life.

Many parents, and even some teachers and administrators, regard movement as independent of thought; they see the mind and body as separate entities. Many of these same people view physical education as a waste of school time and resources. If physical education is taught developmentally, cognitive and affective learning should be explicitly planned for. Teachers should remind parents, educators, and especially students that cognition (particularly analysis, synthesis, and evaluation) is an ongoing part of movement. This is especially true as children

apply basic skills to such complex situations as games, sports, and dances. In teaching the movement alphabet plan to include one or more of the following thinking skills: classification, or grouping; seriation; spatial relations; temporal relations; observation and analysis; problem solving; goal setting; decision-making that involves choosing among alternatives; identifying relationships and patterns; drawing if-then conclusions logically; and understanding cause-and-effect relationships.

We use a combination of informal and formal techniques (McGee, 1984) to consider whether children understand a movement concept or motor skill. The most obvious informal method is to analyze the children's movement responses to see if they show some ability to integrate thinking and movement. Some children know what to do but cannot make the body perform the intended action efficiently. Ultimately, children should be asked about what they know and understand.

I like to check for understanding by asking children questions before or after they perform a particular movement. It's exciting to see how children make sense of what they are learning.

Directions: Each child receives a copy of this form. Children are then paired to do the assessment. The teacher discusses the importance of peer assessment, asking the children to fill out the partner's name, date, and grade. The children read over and discuss the throwing tasks with the teacher to prevent misunderstandings. Each child will attempt 15 throws against a wall in designated areas. Partners will stand behind the lines on the floor designating appropriate distances. "You are to carefully watch your partner and check yes or no for each task they perform. If your partner is a good thrower in your estimation, also check the category. If you feel your partner needs my help, check the last category. Any questions? At the bottom of the page you can write down suggestions that may help your partner become a better thrower."

Partner's name _____*Sally*_____ Date ___*11/17*___ Grade ____*3rd*____

Your name _____*Mary*_____

Tasks

	Partner assessment			
	Yes	Is a good thrower	No	Needs teacher help
My partner keeps his or her side to the target when throwing.				
– Throw #1 against the wall	✔			
– Throw #2 against the wall	✔			
– Throw #3 against the wall	✔	✔		
My partner steps with the opposite foot.				
– Throw #4 against the wall	✔			
– Throw #5 against the wall	✔			
– Throw #6 against the wall	✔	✔		
My partner was able to hit the wall in the air from				
10 yards (#7)	✔	✔		
15 yards (#8)	✔			
20 yards (#9)			✔	✔
25 yards (#10)			✔	✔
Over 30 yards (#11)			✔	✔
My partner hit the target (baseball glove) from				
5 yards (#12)	✔			
10 yards (#13)			✔	✔
15 yards (#14)			✔	✔
20 yards (#15)			✔	✔

Other suggestions for my partner to become a better thrower: _____

_____

_____

Figure 5.6 Partner assessment using the Spring Training learning experience for grades 2–3 (see chapter 9).

Often they will demonstrate creative responses to my movement challenges. For example, I may ask children why the step pattern is so important in manipulation. During a discussion (closure assessment) with a group of fourth graders, I asked the children why it is important to step and swing (learnable piece) when using a long implement for striking. After considering a host of responses—some good, others somewhat illogical—Maria said, "I think it gives you more power to hit the ball farther." This child was at a beginning level as a striker but understood the importance of an efficient swing.

We have to recognize children's learning styles to help them focus on their strengths. The integration of thinking, feeling, and moving will come with time and practice. Mentally practicing the learnable pieces improves the chances for mature movement forms. It is important for children to summarize verbally and in writing what they learn during a lesson or series of lessons.

A more formal technique for assessing understanding is using brief written tests (multiple choice, matching, true or false, and essay items) before and after a lesson. Hensley et al. (1987) report that fewer than half of physical education teachers use written tests of knowledge, and 25% never use written tests of understanding. Figures 5.7 and 5.8 provide ideas about constructing paper-and-pencil items.

A third technique for cognitive assessment is to use index cards to have students answer *one* important question about the learnable pieces within a lesson. The teacher can ask the question aloud or have the children read from the chalkboard or newsprint. For example, I might ask children to describe or draw a leap on their index card. I would then be looking primarily for the takeoff with one foot, landing on the opposite foot, temporary suspension, and light, yielding landings. It's helpful to have the pencils and index cards away from the play area.

A fourth way of testing knowledge and understanding involves using drawings, photos, or videotapes of people performing the motor skills. Questions can be asked about the performer's movement ability, relating it to the lesson's focus. I think it is wise for children to observe mature patterns; however there is also value, for purposes of comparison, in children analyzing inefficient or beginning patterns. Graham (1992) suggests using poker chips to survey the class's understanding. For example, a check for understanding might include a teacher demonstration of both an efficient and an inefficient

running pattern. The children would observe both demonstrations and place a red poker chip in a box indicating the correct pattern. Whatever test is used, it should measure how children understand the differences between and within the movement alphabet and it should distinguish between efficient and inefficient movement.

Affective Assessment

Teachers should design activities that activate the affective domain, the area of learning involving a child's attitudes, beliefs, feelings, interests, values, and social behaviors such as cooperation and leadership. When children demonstrate an active interest in the motor skills they exhibit affective learning. Often a creative shape or response to a movement challenge provides a clue; some children tell you about their pleasure in running, catching, throwing, or different levels of movement. Siedentop (1991) contends that a physical educator's central role is to help students learn how to play and to value physical activity.

Teachers should probe student feelings about the movement alphabet; these feelings can provide rich data for students, parents, and teachers. Information can be collected using anecdotal writing, class discussion, artwork, diaries, and the Likert scale (smiley face) surveys. Measuring positive experiences are at the heart of affective learning.

One assessment technique is a simple paper-and-pencil survey (Graham, 1992; Graham et al., 1993) asking children a series of questions about a particular movement concept or motor skill. They give yes, no, disagree, neutral, and agree (smiley face) responses (see Figure 5.9). I become concerned when some children dislike learning in the gymnasium. Frequent no or disagree responses tell me it is time for dialogue about the importance of learning. Sometimes children need to refocus on the importance of the movement alphabet and overcome negative attitudes.

A second assessment technique uses student diaries, logs, and journals. Children write down important feelings that can provide the teacher with a running account of their perceptions about the subject matter. Because the movement alphabet is the basis for all subsequent physical education, it is important to monitor a child's self-esteem during the elementary years. In the primary grades, when clear writing is difficult,

Understanding Kicking

Directions: Circle the best answer.

1. When learning to kick a ball, you should
   a. move only your legs
   b. step into the kick
   c. wait for the ball to hit your foot
   d. I don't know

2. When learning to become a better kicker, you should use the
   a. toe of the foot
   b. instep (shoe laces)
   c. heel of the foot
   d. I don't know

3. Watching the ball when kicking will
   a. improve your accuracy and direction
   b. prevent your foot from hitting the ground
   c. show that you follow teacher directions
   d. I don't know

4. When kicking for distance, you should "swing through," using the
   a. hip
   b. ankle
   c. knee
   d. I don't know

5. When punting, it is important to
   a. throw the ball in the air and kick it
   b. drop the ball slightly
   c. move your body forward very quickly
   d. I don't know

Figure 5.7   Multiple choice assessment.

Hopping

Directions: Circle the best answer.

1.	Hopping is performed using both feet.	T	F
2.	Hopping requires good balance.	T	F
3.	Rabbits hop.	T	F
4.	Your legs do all the work when hopping.	T	F
5.	The foot is flat when landing after a hop.	T	F

Figure 5.8   True or false assessment.

small discussion circles are helpful. I ask open-ended questions such as, How did you feel about jumping today? What did you like and dislike about jumping? Is jumping important for you to learn? How did you and your partner work together with jumping in unison? The responses can provide data about my teaching effectiveness. Writing and discussion circles are good avenues to express—and get recognition for—positive feelings and even the rapture of physical education. Through them, in short, teachers allow the children time to reflect on their learning.

Lesson Theme: Throwing and Catching

Directions: Circle or shade in the best answer.

1. Throwing and catching are my favorite skills.	Y	N	
2. Throwing is easy for me.	Y	N	
3. Practicing my catching is enjoyable.	Y	N	
4. I practice throwing in my free time.	Y	N	
5. Throwing will help me when I get older.	Y	N	
6. How do you feel about your ability to catch a ball?	☹	☺	☺
7. How do you feel about your ability to throw a ball?	☹	☺	☺
8. How do you feel about your ability to throw a ball under pressure?	☹	☺	☺
9. When the ball is thrown to me in a game, I feel . . .	☹	☺	☺
10. Learning to be good at throwing is important to me.	☹	☺	☺

Figure 5.9   Affective paper-and-pencil survey.

Summary

My friend Tish (see chapter 1) had difficulty learning to kick. His motor skill was not assessed and developmental data were not collected, so he and his parents understood little of their importance. His secondary teachers probably knew very little about what he could and couldn't do when he entered high school. He had only a physical fitness score and maybe a series of grades in physical education, not enough for guidance. What if we assessed a child only on the basis of one standardized reading test and a subjective evaluation of reading aloud? It would be very difficult to adjust instruction and challenge children with appropriate literature. Most classroom teachers know that without frequent and multi-dimensional data collection, it becomes nearly impossible to improve a child's reading skills.

Some physical educators rely solely on physical fitness testing and subjective impressions of a child's movement ability, although many strategies are available for practical and informative assessment. A developmentally appropriate physical education experience for children pays ongoing attention to collecting data about how children participate in class activities. The areas to assess include psychomotor, cognitive, and affective learning (has, is, does; knows; and values) in view of the outcomes of the physically educated person (Franck et al., 1991). I hope this chapter has demystified why and how to assess children who are learning the movement alphabet.

Part II

Teaching Developmentally Appropriate Learning Experiences in Movement Concepts and Skills

The second part of the book includes four chapters that describe in detail how the content might be developed for teaching children. Each chapter consists of a number of learning experiences (LEs) from which lessons can be developed. From each LE, for example, you might be able to develop two or more lessons depending on your teaching situation. It is important to realize, however, that in many instances if one were to teach an entire LE as a lesson, the children would no doubt finish confused—and probably frustrated—because LEs contain far more than can be reasonably taught, and learned, in one 30-minute experience. Most LEs contain several objectives. For most lessons you will want to select one, maybe two, objectives to concentrate on. In other words, you want to pick a "learnable piece" that children can truly understand and grasp—rather than simply exposing them to ideas that can't be understood, let alone learned, in the time allotted.

The learning experiences in Part II are organized according to a similar format. This format is as follows:

- The *Name* of the learning experience
- *Prerequisites*, or skills (if appropriate), children should have already met in order to be the most successful with the learning experience
- *Objectives* that explain the psychomotor, cognitive, and affective skills children will improve as a result of participating in this learning experience. When appropriate, the NASPE benchmarks that these objectives are helping students meet are referenced in parentheses at the end of an objective. The first numbers refer to the grade level the benchmark is found under in the official NASPE document, and the second gives the number of the benchmark itself.
- A *Suggested Grade Range* for the learning experience
- The *Organization* that children will be working in during the learning experience
- The kinds and amounts of *Equipment Needed* for presenting this learning experience to children

- A *Description* of the total learning experience, explained as if the physical education teacher was actually presenting the learning experience to children (additional information for teachers is set off in brackets)
- *Look For*, which gives key points for teachers to keep in mind when informally observing children's progress in the learning experience. These are related to the objectives for the LE.
- *How Can I Change This?*, which allows you to either increase or decrease the difficulty level of the learning experience, thus allowing for all students to be challenged at their ability levels
- *Teachable Moments*, those perfect opportunities either during or after a lesson to discuss how a cognitive or affective concept is related to what has occurred in the learning experience

As a teacher-educator I have struggled to help novice and veteran teachers create learning experiences that are developmentally appropriate for children. All teachers wrestle with this question: How do I teach (plan, implement, and evaluate) the movement concepts and motor skills to children? For years I thought that "canned lessons" violated the art of teaching and the underlying differences in how individuals learn. I argued that formulas limit a teacher's ability to adapt learning tasks to the needs and aptitudes of individual students. Teaching children to be skillful movers is not like baking cookies from a mix! There are no tried-and-true recipes that everyone can follow. Over the years, however, I have observed how the complexity of the learning process baffles us, to the point that many teachers resort to what is most convenient and possibly to 20-fun-games-and-sports. My thinking has changed. I now believe that teachers, regardless of experience, need clear models, or sample learning experiences, that may stimulate ever more creative ways to teach children the movement alphabet.

The next four chapters address the four categories of movement concepts and the two categories of motor skills. Learning experiences for body and space awareness comprise chapter 6, and LEs for effort and relationship concepts are in chapter 7. Chapter 8 includes the locomotor and nonlocomotor patterns and chapter 9 gives learning experiences for the manipulative patterns. Sample learning experiences are only a starting point toward becoming a master teacher. They are not a curriculum to follow rigidly from the first, nor are they an exhaustive treatment of the movement concepts and motor skills. LEs are not recipes that can apply easily to all children in all situations. The value of the LEs lies in their being developmentally appropriate *images* of what elementary physical education can be. I have relied heavily on the *Developmentally Appropriate Physical Education Practices for Children* (Council on Physical Education for Children, 1992), NASPE outcomes (Franck et al., 1991), American Master Teacher Program videotapes, two specialists who teach children on a daily basis, and my own experiences teaching children.

The LEs are designed for children at different developmental levels and for both novice and veteran teachers. The movement concepts are presented first because they can be used to vary motor skills later, or, on their own, become the focus of a learning experience. The LEs in this book will combine well with the LEs in the other content books for games (Belka, 1994), gymnastics (Werner, 1994), dance (Purcell, 1994), and fitness (Ratliffe & Ratliffe, 1994). Together they present a vision of what I consider to be high-quality elementary physical education.

Clearly, even several LEs on one motor skill—kicking, for example—will not produce a mature motor pattern in most children; the LE should not be used repeatedly until children reach high levels of proficiency. Any one learning experience, using the same tasks and teaching methods, will bore children and sour their interest in moving efficiently. The ideas are offered simply as pathways to stimulate you to think and plan. Your curriculum and daily lessons ideally should go beyond these LEs.

Chapter 6

Learning Experiences for Body and Space Awareness

This chapter includes seven learning experiences within the large category of movement concepts. Developed for the subcategories of body and space awareness, these LEs focus on the areas of body parts, pathways, body shapes, self- and general space, twisting and spinning, and directions. The following outline provides a glance at the areas of focus and suggested grade range of the seven LEs.

Focus	Name	Suggested grade range
Body parts	Anatomy	Pre-K–1
Pathways	Trails and Roads	Pre-K–1
Body shapes	Movement Shapes	Pre-K–1
Self-space	Staying at Home	1–2
General space	Painting Movement Pictures	1–2
Twisting and spinning	Twisting and Spinning	3–4
Directions	Directional Gymnastics	3–4

ANATOMY

Objectives

As a result of participating in this learning experience, children will improve their ability to

- Move in isolation and combine body parts in personal and general space while maintaining body balance (K, #7; K, #18)
- Work with a partner while moving various body parts

Suggested Grade Range

Primary (Pre-K–1)

Organization

Self- and general space in a large area with boundaries

Equipment Needed

Carpet square (self-space) for each child, drum, music (your choice), and player

Description

"Find a personal space [carpet] to stand on and wiggle your hips to the music until it stops—no talking. [Music stops.] My second challenge for you is to move your arms and hands above your head to the music. Can you find more than one way to move those arms and hands above your head? Terrific. [Signal to stop.] Let's watch Carol, Traci, Petey, and Jeff's way to move the arms and hands. [Pinpointing; music stops.]

"Now let's sit on our carpets, close our eyes, and move just our feet until the music stops. [Music stops.] Who remembers which body parts we just moved? Correct, Justin, the hips, arms, hands, and feet. It's important to know that we moved different body parts. We can move some body parts, while others remain still. That's good because it means we are skillful. On the signal, stay in personal space and find a way to move your legs and feet at a low level. Try to keep your head and trunk still. [Signal to stop.] This class is so smart! I noticed crawling, creeping, walking on tiptoes, jumping, and hopping. I want the children with blue eyes to place their carpets next to the wall [repeat for children with brown eyes and green eyes] and come back and find a personal space. Check to see that you are not touching your neighbors or any objects. Let's do this again. When the music begins, find a way to move your legs and feet at a low level in general space. [Look for and reinforce a variety of responses. Check the children's understanding of the concepts as you move around to observe them. Music stops.]

"This time I want every boy and girl to jog or run in a special way. Be careful not to touch your neighbor in general space. Move your feet and legs at a low level and your arms at a medium level. Keep your head still—not stiff—at a high level. [Signal to start and stop.] Let's try this again but jog while you move your arms up and down so they are at the middle and high levels. [Signal to start and stop.]

"I have another exciting way for you to move. This time, when you hear the signal, jump in personal space 5 times. [Signal to stop.] What body parts did we use to make us jump? That's right—our feet, ankles, knees, hips, arms, trunk, and even the head. I am going to make this much harder, so pay careful attention. When you hear the signal, who can jump in personal space and move one elbow at the same time? [Signal to stop.] Both elbows? [Stand back-to-wall and observe elbow movements.] Move one elbow high and keep the other elbow at a medium level. Fantastic!

"Our next activity will be a shoulder dance in personal space. Let's listen to the music first and *think* about ways to move the shoulders. [Music on briefly.] All right, here's your chance to show me what you know about body parts. When the music begins, show me how your shoulders can dance at high and medium levels. Don't worry if your head moves too. There is no wrong way to do this. [Music on. Look at shoulders (learnable piece).]

"Let's make this even more fun. Pick a partner; you have exactly 10 seconds to sit down, so that I know you are ready. You and your partner will find three ways to match or mirror your shoulders. This means your shoulders move the same way, at the same speed, and in the same direction. See if you can match or mirror how your legs move. Now practice quickly for awhile. [Signal to start and stop.] Our final task will be to move the head and arms to the music. You do not have to match head and arm movements with your partner but you are still working together. [Music on, circulate to observe, music stops.]

"Let's gather in a circle and talk about what we have learned today. What body parts did we move today? Yes, we moved our heads, shoulders, elbows, hands, hips, knees, ankles, feet, and toes. In what kinds of space did these body parts move? Yes, Brett, we moved in self-space and in general space. Who knows why we want to control our body parts? Yes, they help us when we work and play. When we write, our fingers, hands, arm, eyes, and even the head might move, but the rest of the body stays quiet. When we jump and run, some parts of the body have to move in certain ways. We need to feel and know what the body is doing while it moves. As we line up, let's keep our lips and mouth quiet, and think to ourselves about the body parts and muscles that are moving to get us from our circle to the doorway. Great job, children."

Look For

- Can the children identify each body part?
- Can the children distinguish between the three levels: high, medium, low?
- Can the children keep their balance while moving in personal and general space?
- Can the children move combinations of body parts while others remain still?

How Can I Change This?

- Have the children move a yarn ball with various body parts.
- Have the children point to different body parts.
- Have the children use hula hoops to practice moving various body parts.
- Have the children attempt to balance on different body parts.
- Ask the children to travel across the general space using only their legs.
- Combine the body part movements with directions and pathways.
- Have the children spend more time with partners to find more ways that body parts can move. Have them make body shapes or statues at different levels.

TEACHABLE MOMENTS

Use an action figure (Barbie or GI Joe) to demonstrate body parts moving at different levels.

Have the children make the letters *C*, *J*, *O*, and *X* with their arms and legs at low, medium, and high levels.

Have children name which body part they use when tapping a balloon in self-space.

TRAILS AND ROADS*

Objectives

As a result of participating in this learning experience, children will improve their ability to

- Distinguish between straight, curved, and zigzag pathways while traveling (K, #4)
- Move in various pathways
- Apply the pathways in daily life

Suggested Grade Range

Primary (Pre-K–1)

Organization

Large open space (gym floor, playground) with pathways marked on the floor with tape or colored chalk (see Figure 6.1)

Equipment Needed

Colored tape or chalk

Description

"On the floor there are pathways. Which is the pathway you used coming to PE class? Was it straight? Did you see a colored tape? A pathway is the trail your body uses to get from one place to another place. We will be practicing many different pathways today. [Divide children into equal groups.] First, find a pathway with your group and then quietly wait there for instructions—ready, go. [Signal to stop.] When you travel backward, it's best if you look *over* one shoulder and then over the other shoulder [teacher demonstrates]. Ready, go. [Signal to stop.] Now I would like your group to

Figure 6.1 Sample trails and roads.

*This learning experience was contributed by Vanessa Bryan, an elementary specialist at Durham Elementary School, Durham, California.

find another pathway to practice on. Ready, go. That was a great job moving without crashing or bumping into anyone. Remember our low, medium, and high levels? Yes. I would like you to practice the different levels on your pathways. Ready, go. [Signal to stop.]

"Now you can change the way you travel along your pathway. You could hop, leap, run, gallop, slide, skip, and jump. Pick three different ways to travel along your pathway. Ready, go. [Signal to stop.] I would like you to find a different pathway to travel on, one you haven't tried yet. Ready, go. Look at your pathway. If the pathway could make a sound, what sound would it make? Oh—good sounds! Travel on your pathway carefully, making your pathway sound. Ready, go. [Signal to stop.]

"We have many pathways to think about. If your pathway looks like a lot of Zs, it's called a *zigzag*. If it circles around, or part of the way around, it's called *curved*. If it has no twists or turns, it is *straight*. I want you to travel on your pathway the way you like most. I will come around to watch you and ask you what kind of pathway you're on. Ready, go. [Signal to stop.] Now, children, sit down on your pathway. When we're at school and we walk from the cafeteria to the library or to the office, are there colored tapes on the floor to show us the way? No. But we do use pathways to get to all those places, right? Yes. If you wanted to go to the library from your classroom, could you walk in only a straight pathway? No, you'd run into the wall! That's right, Amy, you have to turn a corner at the office and then at the double doors. When you go home today, from school, see what kind of pathways you use. You did good work today. Remember trails, roads, and pathways."

Look For

- Can the students follow the taped pathway correctly and without losing balance?
- Can the students differentiate clearly between curved, straight, and zigzag pathways?
- Can the students make sharp turns and change direction on a zigzag pathway?

How Can I Change This?

- Have the students create their own pathways.
- Have the students practice leading and following with a partner.

TEACHABLE MOMENTS

Make a map of the school on a portable chalkboard to show various common pathways.

Display the pathway vocabulary on a poster board.

Have the students draw a map from the classroom to the gymnasium, indicating the pathways they take.

Have the students run the bases on a softball diamond, and then discuss with them the pathways they have taken.

MOVEMENT SHAPES

Objectives

As a result of participating in this learning experience, children will improve their ability to

- Make body shapes (curved, narrow, wide, twisted) (K, #14)
- Understand that different body shapes are important for sports, games, exercise, and dance (1–2, #23)

Suggested Grade Range

Primary (Pre-K–1)

Organization

Self- and general space in a large area with boundaries

Equipment Needed

Carpet squares; drum, M.C. Hammer or other rap recording, record or tape player; pictures of dancers and male and female athletes

Description

"Children, find a personal space [carpet] to stand on. Freeze! As you stand on the carpet, notice that your body makes a shape. Everyone is standing up, but look around the room and see how we have different body shapes. Some of us are tall, some of us round, some of us short, and some of us are thin. What's really exciting about movement is that we can create body shapes to use to do different things. Today we are going to experiment with making all kinds of body shapes. We will work with wide shapes, curved shapes, narrow shapes, and twisted shapes in our personal spaces. On the signal, show me how you can make the shape of a table with your body. [Stop on signal.] Show me now if you can make the shape of a banana with your body. [Stop.] Show me how you can make a telephone pole with your body. [Stop.] Finally, show me how you make the shape of a pretzel with your body. Please stay in your space. You can giggle, but no talking or falling down. [Stop.]

"Even though the shapes we are making with our bodies are funny, it will be important to make many different shapes as we perform various movements in physical education. Now, let's try these same shapes—wide, curved, narrow, twisted—at different levels (low, medium, high). [Stop.] When I give you the signal, we will begin to make these shapes in order, or sequence. We will go in this order: wide, curved, narrow, twisted. You make a different body shape each time I hit the drum. [Drum beats, then stop.]

"This time, let's use the general space and travel on the signal, but you must make a different shape each time you hear the sound. No talking while moving. [Drum beats, then stop.] You are beginning to get the idea that our body parts can make many interesting shapes and forms. As you move in general space, concentrate on making rounded shapes by curving your spine. Freeze! This time, show me some twisted shapes with your legs at a low level in personal space. Think of your legs being tied in knots. [Stop.] Now show me a shape you've never been in before, in your whole life. [Signal to stop.]

"Come, children, gather around me so we can talk awhile. Look at these four pictures. This is Patrick Ewing, who plays basketball with the New York Knicks. He is guarding an opponent—see what a wide shape he makes? This is the Hammer, dancing in a curved shape. This third picture is Kim Zmeskal doing a handstand. See how it is a narrow shape? My fourth picture is Will Clark from the Texas Rangers, hitting a ball in a twisted shape. Let's see if we can remember their shapes. Changing your body shape is important for becoming a good mover. Let's go back to our personal spaces and try some more shapes. Think about how we can move our body parts into different positions.

"On the signal, let's pretend we are swimming in the pool—you can swim at any level. Show me the shape your body would take. [Stop.] Now let's pretend we are ice skaters, moving in general space. How would an ice skater move and what body shapes would I see? [Stop.]

"Listen to this rap music by M.C. Hammer; some of you may have heard it before. We are going to make different curved and twisted shapes, in personal space, when the music begins. There are many good ways to make a shape. Now, no falling down or talking, so that everyone can hear the music. [Play tape or CD, then stop.] I like the different shapes you showed me with your bodies as I walked around the room. Let's ask this half of the class [half watch, half move] to make some more shapes to the same music. Watch all the creative ways they make shapes with their bodies. [Play tape or CD, then stop.]

"Today we made hundreds of different body shapes using our arms, legs, heads, torsos, necks, and feet. We can use all these body shapes in the future. What shapes did we practice today? Right, Paula, wide is one shape. What were the others? Thanks, Sean, Maria, and Billy for remembering narrow, curved, and twisted. Why is it important to move our bodies in different shapes? Your answer is right on, Matilda; different activities need different body shapes. Sometimes you have to create a shape to solve a problem. Do you see how we could use these shapes in sports, games, dance, and exercise? One example would be the goalie making a wide shape to block someone who tries a shot on the goal. There are many others as we begin to think about how we move. Your homework is to bring me four pictures of people using our four body shapes (wide, curved, narrow, twisted). You might look at some old newspapers and magazines to find your pictures. Here are some examples. I look forward to seeing the body shapes you make the next time we meet."

Look For

- Can the children clearly distinguish between the four shapes?
- Do they curl the spine when making rounded shapes?
- Can the children sequence the shapes following the drum beat?
- Do the children understand that body shapes apply to sports, games, dance, and exercise?
- Did the children just bounce and laugh during the music, or did they perform twisted and curved shapes in personal space? (Figure 6.2)

How Can I Change This?

- Travel and freeze in different body shapes, without falling.
- Introduce symmetrical and asymmetrical shapes.
- Have the children work with partners creating statues.
- Have the children try to make shapes in flight.

Figure 6.2   Look for children performing twisted and curved shapes.

TEACHABLE MOMENTS

Use photographs of proficient performers depicting different shapes.

Teach the vocabulary *wide, curved, narrow, twisted*.

Have the children make shapes with a partner. Making letters and numbers is a good starting point. Praise cooperative behavior and teamwork.

STAYING AT HOME

Objectives

As a result of participating in this learning experience, children will improve their ability to

- Move in self-space without touching other people or objects
- Manipulate an object in self-space
- Move in self-space as a precursor for games, sports, dance, and exercise (1–2, #23)

Suggested Grade Range

Primary (1–2)

Organization

Large bounded area

Equipment Needed

1 sheet of newspaper for each child (22" × 27"), drum, picture of a house, 10 pylons

Description

"Good afternoon boys and girls. Children, find a newspaper [scattered on the ground] to sit on. All of you know how it feels to stay at home [show picture of a house]. Today, the newspaper is your home. Be very careful with your home, because it can become ripped or torn if you are not careful. All of our movement activities will take place here. We call this home a *self-space*. Your desk in the classroom is your self-space, or home. Our first challenge is to see if you can place your entire body inside your house. [Signal to start and stop.] Now find a second way to fit your body into the house, different from the first. Be sure to keep your arms and legs in close. [Signal to start and stop.]

"This time I want you to stretch your body as wide as possible, in the house, but choose either a high or low level. Great. Now, see if you can keep the trunk of your body inside the house, but your legs and arms can hang outside the windows and doors. [Signal to start and stop.] I noticed you used some very creative ways to solve the problem. This time, let's make a chair with your body to fit inside the house. Wow—look at all your different kinds of chairs. Now make a table for the house. A bed; a refrigerator; a couch; a lamp; a tall plant. Fantastic!

"It's time to explore the basement, the roof, and other parts of the house—please be careful not to tear it. [Move around to observe how children are exploring their spaces.] Let's spend some time outside the house. Keep one arm in the house but move your body outside it. [Signal to start and stop.] Now, keep one foot in the house but move the rest of your body outside the house. You will need to twist and turn or bend and stretch. You're so smart. Let's try both feet in the house and both hands outside the house. [Signal to start and stop.] Who can find a way to build a bridge with your body over the house? [Signal to stop.]

"Each of you has a front yard, a backyard, and two side yards. You may explore those spaces, but don't get into your neighbor's yard. [Signal to start and stop.] The yard around your house goes only as far as your neighbor's property, and we do not allow fences in this subdivision. I want you to skip or hop in your yard only and not in the house. [Signal to start and stop.] Probably you can make only one or two steps in each direction in your yard. This time I want you to move around your house at a low level. Now move more slowly. OK, now let's jog around the house 5 times without touching it. [Signal to start and stop.] Now we will try something only Superhumans can do: Jump over the house—be careful not to land on it!—and be sure to land on your feet. [Signal to start and stop.] I really liked the way you stayed in your own yard.

"This time I want everyone to leave their houses on the signal [drumbeat] and walk through your street in the neighborhood, but you cannot touch the neighbors' houses, and you must return quickly, without touching, when the drum beats a second time. Remember to stay within the city limits (bounded by the pylons). [Signal to start and stop.] Let's try this again, but this time move a little farther away from your home. You may shake the hand of a neighbor, but you must not talk. Remember where your house is—they all look the same. [Signal to start and stop.]

"Our last activity will test your abilities to understand your home, or self-space. Who knows what a transformer is? Yes, Tonya, there are toys called transformers. With these toys we can change one thing into another. I want you to transform your house into a ball. Go. [Signal to stop.] You can make a better ball out of your house by squeezing the paper tightly—if it comes loose, tighten it again. This time I want you to pretend you are still in your house and move the ball around different body parts. Go. [Signal to stop.] If the ball rolls into the yard, bring it back to the house, or your self-space. Try to keep both your body and your ball in your space. This time, toss and catch the ball in your imaginary living room. Wait for the signal. If the ball rolls into the yard, or someone else's yard, quickly bring it back. [Signal to start and stop.] Let's try tossing the ball with one hand and catching it with two hands. Remember to keep it in your own self-space. [Signal to start and stop.]

"Now, deposit your balls into the trash can and sit beside me without touching each other. Thank you, boys and girls, for following my directions so carefully today. Now that you are sitting in your own self-space, let me ask you some questions. What did you learn to do today? No, Chelsea, we did not really learn to play catch. Who else knows? Correct, Juan, we moved in our own self-space, or house. Yes, Fran, we learned to move in our self-space without touching anyone else. This is important for many games, sports, exercises, and dances.

"Raise your hand if you know what a batter's box is in baseball. Raise your hand if you know where the goalie can go in soccer. Raise your hand if you have ever been bowling. All of these activities require understanding home, or self-space. Sometimes there are certain places where you *must* move and other places where you are not allowed. Sometimes you can leave home, like the goalie in soccer, but then you must always come back to protect the goal. The pitching mound was my home when I played baseball as a youngster. I had to start from the pitching rubber each time I threw the ball. Batters have self-spaces too—in one game, I stepped out of the batter's box, and the umpire called me out for leaving my space. I hope this never happens to you. It won't if you can move your body in a limited area. This is called your home, or self-space, in physical education. See you Tuesday for our self-space activity using jump ropes."

Look For

- Do the children stay close to the newspaper while moving?

- Do the children avoid touching neighbors while moving?

- Do the children remain in self-space while removing their marker (transforming the newspaper house into a ball)?

- Are the children able to concentrate, moving without talking?

- Are children frequently checking their self-space as they move?

How Can I Change This?

- Use ropes, hula hoops, carpets, poly-spots (rubber circles for marking self-space), and yarn balls for manipulation.
- Have children make narrow, wide, twisted, and rounded shapes in self-space.
- Have children try other forms of locomotion around or over their self-space.
- Have partners work together to strike a balloon in self-space.

TEACHABLE MOMENTS

Teach the vocabulary *self-* and *general space.*

Ask children five oral questions about the use of self-space. For example: "True or false: (a) In baseball the first baseman covers the entire field. (b) The airline pilot flies the airplane from the cockpit. (c) The secretary types letters while moving around the room."

PAINTING MOVEMENT PICTURES

Objectives

As a result of participating in this learning experience, children will improve their ability to

- Combine motor skills while moving in general space, without touching others
- Anticipate and find the open spaces in the play area
- Move in general space with partner and ball

Suggested Grade Range

Primary (1–2)

Organization

Large bounded area

Equipment Needed

1 ball for each child, drum or other noisemaker as signal, chalkboard or other vehicle to convey this message: Select a ball and practice bouncing it in self-space for 2 minutes. When you hear the signal, the drumbeat, you may bounce it in general space, without talking or touching your neighbors, for 2 minutes. On the third signal, put the ball against the wall and move to the middle of the play space (circle) for additional directions. [Use words, pictures, or a videocassette to communicate this message to the children.]

Description

Children read the chalkboard upon arrival at the play area. "Good afternoon, children. I appreciated your reading today's directions carefully and completing each of the tasks during our warm-up. Have any of you been to an art gallery? Katie, your hand was raised. What kinds of paintings did you see? OK; did any of the artists use only half of the canvas, leaving the rest blank? I didn't think so. A good artist thinks about the image he wants to paint, then usually uses the entire canvas, or space. A good artist uses the middle, the sides, and even the corners. Good dancers also use the entire stage area; basketball players use all of the court; and water polo players use the whole swimming pool. Today we go back to general space and think of ourselves as artists using the entire canvas.

"Find a space on the floor, but don't talk or touch anyone else. When you hear the signal, walk in a variety of directions and pathways to cover the entire canvas of our playing area. [Signal start and stop.] Great job. This time, let's move at different levels. You remember—the choices are high, medium, and low levels. [Signal start and stop.]

"This time I want you to slide around the entire play area. Remember to use your arms, but do not touch your neighbors. [Signal start and stop.] Our next task is to jog in general space. Be careful not to bump other children. You should look for the open space, and move toward these empty spaces in our play area. [Signal to start.] Freeze! That was fine. Let's make this harder. When I give the signal, I want you to run for 15 seconds. Remember to stay within the boundaries, move to the open spaces, and don't touch anyone else. Go! [Signal to stop.] Most of you found the open spaces while running and stayed under control. Terry and Sharon will have to sit out for 1 minute for touching. I am serious about body control in general space. Very few sports, games, dances, and exercises require contact or collisions. This time, find a partner and slide together (you do not have to hold hands) in the general space. [Signal start and stop.]

"Now I want Terry and Sharon to return to our activity and try harder to move carefully. This time get a ball from against the wall and bring it to your self-space. When I give the signal, I want you to juggle the ball, to toss it back and forth, while moving into the open spaces. [Signal start and stop.] The next challenge is to place the ball under your arm. This is what a runner does in football. When you hear the signal, run and dodge the other runners; no stiff arms. [Signal start and stop.] Let's try this one again. As you run, look for the open spaces. You are looking for the end zone. Go! [Stop.] I liked the way some of you used the entire field.

"I have two more tasks for you to show me that you understand general space. First, let's bounce the ball in general space, not losing control of the ball. Remember dribbling from last week? I want you to cover the entire playing area. Go! [Signal to stop.] Our last task is to bounce a ball at the same time as your partner. You may jog, slide, or skip. Be careful not to bump each other, and look for the open spaces. Remember—stay within the boundaries. [Signal start and stop.] Please put the ball back in the barrels and sit beside me without touching your neighbors.

"Today's learning activity was not about football, not about basketball, and not about art. What was the purpose of our movement? That's correct, Julie, we tried to move our bodies in general space. Yes, Danny, we were trying to move in *all* the open spaces. Right, Carlos, we had to stay within the boundaries. That's correct, Chelsea, bumping was *not* OK. Who can think of other sports, games, dances, and exercises where it is important to move in the entire area or general space? Let's write these on the board [soccer, baseball, folk dancing, handball, tennis, etc.]. In most activities we have a limited space. We must learn to move in all the available area, as you did today, and like the artist who paints on the whole canvas."

Look For

- Children who can dodge and use open spaces.
- Children who are tentative and hide on the outside fringes of the boundary area. These children need encouragement to travel in traffic or the middle of the space. Some children already feel comfortable being close to peers, possibly toward the middle of the space, but need encouragement to travel to the sides and outer edges of the boundaries.
- Partners who can work in unison, once most of the children understand general space. Find pairs who are creative, and pinpoint how they are working well.

How Can I Change This?

- Select other combinations of motor skills, such as sliding and striking in general space.
- Have the children demonstrate quick bursts of speed in different directions and using the open spaces.
- Have partners lead and follow as they move.
- Have children get closer and closer to each other, but without touching, performing the locomotor patterns in general space.
- Place obstacles (hoops, carpets, cones, etc.) in the playing area to increase the complexity of moving carefully.

TEACHABLE MOMENTS

Have children trace their movement pathways on index cards; then have partners discuss, demonstrate, and replicate one another's movement sequences.

Show a videotape of skillful soccer players maintaining space, staying within the boundaries, and finding open spaces.

Show the children a tape of proficient basketball players finding open spaces to receive a pass and to shoot from. Some classes may be able to understand the reason for a screen or pick.

TWISTING AND SPINNING

Objectives

As a result of participating in this learning experience, children will improve their ability to

- Demonstrate twisting and spinning movements in self- and general space
- Modify twisting and spinning movements using speed, force, and flow (3–4, #21)
- Understand the application of twisting and spinning movements to games, sports, dance, and exercise

Suggested Grade Range

Intermediate (3–4)

Organization

A large bounded area

Equipment Needed

Carpets or exercise mats for each child, drum, "Twist" by Chubby Checker, "Mexico" by James Taylor, CD or tape player

Description

"Good afternoon, children. Today we will be twisting and spinning. Everyone find a self-space carpet. When you hear the signal, I want you to spin your body on the mat or near the carpet. [Signal to start and stop.] Now I want you to twist your body in self-space. [Signal start and stop.] Now, show me the way you would throw a ball a long distance—imagine from the outfield to home plate in baseball. Try it three times. Let's do it again, but this time add a twist and spin into your throw. Go! [Signal to stop.]

"Come in close to me for discussion. What is the difference between a twist and turn? Those are both good explanations, Lizzy and Bill. More accurately, a twist is moving a body part, like your wrist [demonstrate] around a stationary point. Part of you stays still, while the other part twists around it. Show me how you would "wring out" a wet dish rag as you sit before me. Which part of you turns around, and which parts stay put? A twisting movement can take place at the spine, neck, shoulder, hip, and wrist. These places where bones meet in our body are called joints. Let's try some more movements that involve twisting.

"Try keeping your feet from moving, and twist your trunk and spine to the right. Now twist to the left. [Signal to start and stop.] Our next task is to twist slowly and then quickly. [Start and stop.] Remember to twist and not shake. Now, twist as if you are tied up. Pretend you are a magician trying to untie yourself without the use of your arms. [Signal to start and stop.] Can you twist one body part in one direction, and twist another in the opposite direction? Try it. [Stop.] Can you twist like a slinky or like a telephone cord that is coiled up? How about like a pretzel? [Stop.] Show me how you use the wrists to turn the shower handle on and off. [Stop.] Twist your head around now—how far can you see in the opposite direction? Keep your shoulders still. Now try the different ways you can twist using only the shoulder region. [Signal to stop.]

"Over 30 years ago a man named Chubby Checker was popular because he created a cool song and dance called the "Twist." He thought of the dance after drying off his back with a towel after taking a shower. The movement looks like this. When I play the music, try as many ways as you can think of to twist in self-space. Keep twisting the entire time. [Music—2 minutes on—and off.] Nice job; I think you have the idea. Finally, we will pretend that we are hitting a baseball. Show me how you would strike fastballs 10 times with an imaginary bat. Don't forget to stay in the batter's box, and twist your arms, wrists, and trunk. [Signal start and stop.]

"In self-space, let's try the spinning motion. [Signal start and stop.] Some of you are still twisting. The spinning motion is different. In a spin the whole body moves in a circle. As I spin around [teacher demonstrates a 360-degree spin] my entire body moves in space. Let's all try a full-circle spin. Go! [Stop.] I want you to try it again. This time stay on the ball of one foot. [Teacher demonstration.] The spin will be easier. OK. [Stop.] In your own self-space try a quarter-spin, half-spin, and three-quarter spin; Go! [You may need to demonstrate these fractions. Signal to stop.]

"Now, sit on your carpet, and spin your body around. [Stop.] It's going to get harder. Lie on your stomach, and spin your body. Now the back. [Stop.] Let's try making windmills with the arms. This is twisting—do you see the difference? OK. Think of a clock and go from noon to 11 o'clock. Twist with your arms and shoulders. Now twist the opposite way from 11 to 1. [Stop.] Do you know the underhand softball pitch for speed? Isn't that twisting too? Try it in self-space. [Stop.]

"A few minutes ago we worked on turns and spins, or pivots. Let's try to jump and turn [demonstrate first one-quarter, then one-half.] The trick is to land on your feet and keep your balance. Go! [Signal to stop.] Let's move the carpets away from our general space and return them against the wall. When I give you the signal, travel in general space, but spin each time I beat the drum. [Demonstrate and explain that one beat = quarter-turn; two beats = half-turn; three beats = full, or 360-degree turn. Signals to start and stop.] Let's listen to this music by James Taylor [brief introduction]. Once again you will travel in general space without touching anyone. Every time you hear Mr. Taylor say the country name *Mexico*, you are to turn in self-space, then continue traveling. Any questions? [Music on and off.] Our last challenge is to work with a partner to Mr. Taylor's music. You will travel together and both spin, spinning whole circles or 360-degrees each time the name *Mexico* is used in the song. [Music on and off.] Thank you for your careful work in the last activity. [Children gather near teacher for class closure. Review the following points about twisting and spinning.]

- "Twisting and spinning are movement forms.
- Twisting and spinning are different movements. [Quiz individuals on the distinction between the two movements.]
- A skilled hitter in baseball twists many body parts at the same time. [Teacher demonstration.]
- Who can think of other activities that require twisting and spinning?
- Twisting and spinning require good flexibility." [Quiz students on where and which joints of the body.]

Look For

- Are movement responses clear when children twist and spin?
- Does the body spin for twisting actions?
- Do the children understand what is meant by quarter-, half-, three-quarter, and full turns?

How Can I Change This?

- Guide the children to discover the differences between spinning and twisting with a variety of movement examples.
- Question students on the definitions and spelling of these two terms.
- For children who are ready, use milk crates as a flight base for jumping, landing, spinning, and twisting.

- Combine a run, jump, spin or twist, and landing.
- In cooperative classes have pairs of children lock arms and swing their partners (both right and left, when the name *Mexico* sounds).
- For the twist, partners can try to mirror each other for 15-second intervals during the "Twist."
- Have children twist (with different body parts) while moving in general space.
- Have children twist and spin while chasing, fleeing, and dodging.

TEACHABLE MOMENTS

An action figure or doll can provide a great example of the difference between spinning and twisting.

Have children draw a picture of themselves spinning or twisting. Teach the vocabulary *spinning*, *twisting*.

DIRECTIONAL GYMNASTICS

Prerequisites

- Roll to a one-foot balance
- Jump over an object, land, roll, return to the feet
- Roll, balance, roll
- Run, jump (half-twist), roll backward
- Transfer weight from feet to hands and back to feet
- Balance on three parts (e.g., head, foot, hand)
- Travel in space, stop, balance on three body parts
- Hold an inverted balance for 5 seconds
- Transfer weight from feet to back to feet without using hands

Objectives

As a result of participating in this learning experience, children will improve their ability to

- Use directions purposefully to change the continuity or flow of a gymnastics sequence (3–4, #21)
- Design and practice an educational gymnastics sequence to include the directions *up, down, forward, backward* (3–4, #26)
- Use smooth directional transitions between movements
- Be respectful, considerate, and supportive of other's feelings, skill levels, and cultural values (3–4, #27)

Suggested Grade Range

Intermediate (3–4)

Organization

Scattered formation

Equipment Needed

Mats or carpet squares (1 for every 2 children), 4" × 6" note cards and pencils, 1 handout for each child (see prerequisites list)

Description

The assumption is that children have been working on rolling, balancing, and weight transfer activities as part of an educational gymnastics program (see Werner, 1994).

"Class, let's sit together, without touching or talking. It's great to see you again! Today we will bring together, or consolidate, our learning of the past several weeks. What gymnastics skills have we been working on? Yes, Gayle, rolling, balancing, and weight transfer. We are going to design and practice what we call gymnastics *sequences*. Here is a handout of the major tasks [see prerequisites list] for today's lesson. You are to choose three of the tasks and plan what order to do them in, a sequence showing each movement—forward, backward, sideways, up, and down. The sequence should not last more than 1 minute. A minute sounds short, but you can do a lot in 60 seconds.

"You need to think through the sequence and show it on these cards. I will ask you to demonstrate your routine toward the end of the period. It will be important for you to perform each of the movements and show directional changes, so I will give you lots of practice time. Are there questions? Yes, Glenn, you may include more than three tasks if you wish, but I will be looking primarily for control, careful transitions from one movement to the other, and of course all the directional changes.

"Please share a mat or grassy space with a partner. You may need to help each other after you have designed your sequence. I will circulate and help you design the best possible sequences. Raise your hand if you need help along the way. Any other questions? Let's do it. Begin by thinking, then write down your movements, and then put them together. [The children should follow with practicing and refining the sequences. Remind them that they will demonstrate their sequences to the class.]

"I like the way you are practicing and staying on task. I can't wait to see your final product. [After 20 to 25 minutes ask the children to perform their sequences. Choose half of the class to observe while the other half performs.] Those of you who are observing, please pick out one performer and watch for the directional changes we discussed. First group, start when you're ready. [The first group finishes their routines.] Let's show our appreciation for the creative movements we just watched [applaud]. Now the second group will perform. Pick out only one performer to watch and see how he or she changes directions. [Action completed.] Fantastic.

"Our final challenge will be to work in a different way with your partners. You will swap sequences [cards]. Without telling your partner anything, see if they can first figure out and perform your routine. If they have difficulty understanding your routine, discuss and teach them the best way you know how. Maybe I will discover some future physical education teachers. It's important, when you teach someone, to be respectful, considerate, and supportive of your partner's ideas and feelings. [Teacher circulates to assist partners and observe the cooperative skills.]

"I need the partners to work together to place the mats in a stack for the next class. Then come sit beside me. What were our objectives today? Yes, Maria, we wanted to perform at least three gymnastics movements to include the directions of forward, backward, sideways, up, and down. Now for the more difficult question: Why is it important for you to choose directional movements well for performing games, dances, sports, and gymnastics? You're on the right track, Lisa. We're always making decisions about where to move in space. It's important to know your directional options. Your choices make the difference between a beautiful movement that shows body control, and a so-so or just OK movement. Sometimes directional choices will produce a goal, a point, a run, or just a good feeling inside that you have been creative. Thanks for the creative sequences and for the cooperation each of you demonstrated. Please hand me your cards, with your names on them, before you leave."

Look For

- Smooth directional transitions between movements that you should encourage. Some children will need assistance, even though they do not ask for it.

- Creative thinking and movement in the design (cards) and routines (see Figure 6.3)

- The child's ability to solve the movement problems individually. The less talking, the better during the design stage of the routines.

How Can I Change This?

- If children are ready, have them design their sequence to include an approach (beginning point), middle portion, and a final shape (ending point).

- Use music with the routines.

- Have partners develop sequences together.

- Teach the children a notation system (see Steve Sanders's gymnastic notation described in Graham et al., 1987).

Figure 6.3   Look for creative thinking and movement as children design their routines.

TEACHABLE MOMENTS

Focus on the process of partners working together for the final task.
Show children how crucial directional changes are in sports, games, and dances by using videotapes of skillful performers.
As homework, have each child design and practice another sequence for the next class period.

Chapter 7

Learning Experiences for Effort and Relationship Concepts

This chapter includes five learning experiences within the category of movement concepts. LEs have been developed for the subcategories of speed, relationships to objects or others, force, relationship to a partner, and flow. The following outline provides a glance at the focus and the suggested grade range of each LE.

Focus	Name	Suggested grade range
Speed	Turtles and Rabbits	Pre-K–1
Relationships to objects or others	Hoops and Me	Pre-K–1
Force	Only the Strong and Light Survive	1–2
Relationship to a partner	Moving Scarves	3–4
Flow	Sentence Scrabble	3–4

TURTLES AND RABBITS

Objectives

As a result of participating in this learning experience, children will improve their ability to

- Demonstrate clear contrasts between fast and slow speeds as they travel (K, #3)
- Distinguish between sudden movements and sustained movements in personal and general space
- Understand that fast movements may hinder one's ability to accomplish a movement task (1–2, #23)

Suggested Grade Range

Primary (Pre-K–1)

Organization

Self-space and general space in a large bounded area

Equipment Needed

Hula hoops (self-space), drum, pictures of airplanes on large cards (see Figure 7.1)

Description

Children are seated around the teacher. "Who knows Aesop's fable about the tortoise and the hare? What is a tortoise? How about a hare? How are these two animals different? [Briefly discuss the fable and how the two animals differ in speed.] Today we are going to move our bodies slow like the turtle and fast like the rabbit. I need each of you to move slowly to a hula hoop without touching anyone else. [Signal start and stop.] I liked the ways you demonstrated slow movement. Many of you understand how the turtle moves. How slowly can you move one body part in your hoop? [Signal.] Let's try another body part different from the first one you chose. [Signal.] Now let's try one more body part that nobody has moved slowly yet. [Signal.] Great job. Let's try some fast movements like the rabbit. When I hit the drum, show me a sudden movement with one body part. [Signal start and stop. Repeat using other body parts.] Now when you hear the drum show me quick movements with two body parts. [Signal start and stop.] Now let's try three body parts. [Check for understanding. Signal start and stop.] Find a way to move your entire body quickly for 10 seconds on the signal. I will tell you when time is up. [Signal start and stop.] Wonderful.

[Put hoops away and direct children to find self-space.] "When I give you the signal, show me with your body how a windmill might move on a day without wind. [Signal start and stop.] Who can make their body move like an old person crossing the street? You can move in general space to do this. [Signal start and stop.] Let's pretend you are an old car that hardly works. How would it move without touching other cars in the parking lot, our general space? [Signal start and stop.] If you were holding the hand of a baby, how would you move quickly so that the baby wouldn't fall? [Signal start and stop.]

"Could you run that fast, Tommy, or would the baby fall down and cry? Sometimes we have to move slowly or someone could get hurt. Let's try this one: In your own space show me with your body how a popsicle would melt on a warm day. Great. We should try this one more time. [Stop.] How would you walk on a balance beam this high [shoulder level of the teacher] in the Olympics so that you didn't fall off and lose points

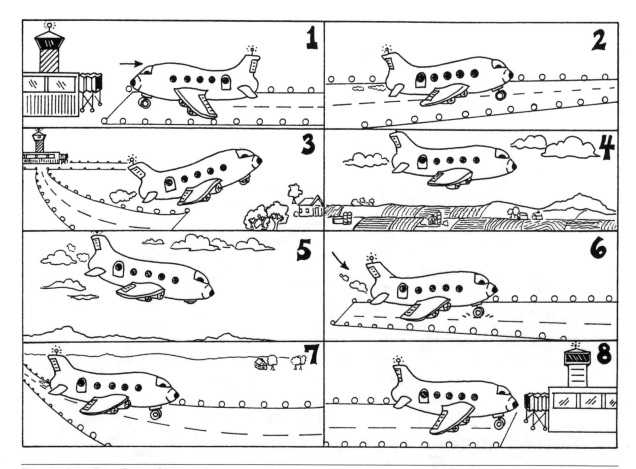

Figure 7.1 Sample airplane cards.

from the judges? [Signal start and stop.] How fast would you run if you had to run for a whole hour? Show me. [Signal start and stop.] No, Taneesha, you couldn't run that fast for a whole hour without stopping. You would run out of energy unless you were in great shape.

"Remember what happened to the hare? He ran so fast he tired out and took a nap, and of course the tortoise with the slow and steady pace passed him. The word pace means the rate of speed. Listen to me beat the drum at different speeds. Great job, class. Now let's pretend your body is a motorcycle. When the drum beats slowly, you are traveling near a school and must go slowly because children are around. When the drum beats a little faster, pretend you are on a road with traffic moving more quickly. Then when the drum beats really fast, you are zipping along out on the highway. Remember these rules: No one can pass the speed limit, no one can fall or wreck the motorcycle, and no one can touch another motorcycle. There will be a penalty if any of these things happens, plus your license will be taken away [time-out]. [Signal start and stop.] I liked the ways your motorcycles showed changing speeds on different streets and highways. This time when you hear the signal to stop, show me a sudden stop without falling or crashing. [Signal start and stop.] Wow, this class is so skillful—you are really getting the idea of changing speeds.

"I have one more task that will be your final test. I will be watching you very closely to see if you understand how to change speeds. You're going to pretend you are an airplane. First you will back up away from the gate very slowly, then you move forward to the runway, going the speed of a slow-moving car, and get ready to take off. You fly 400 miles an hour—very, very fast. Then you descend, or come down out of the air; put down your wheels, land slowly, and come to a complete stop. In pretend time, the flight will be about 2 hours long [2 minutes]. Watch the picture cards to see how fast you should be going. I will be the air traffic controller; you must follow my directions or I will have to take away your pilot's license [give a time-out]. [Run through the sequence of eight cards with pictures attached.] Thank you pilots, nice flight. You can park your jets close to me, but don't touch.

[Children sit in a circle around the teacher.] "Raise your hand if you remember how we moved our bodies today. There are many hands up, so I will pick Jessica today. Yes, Jessica, we were moving our bodies both fast and slow. What story or fable reminds you that fast is not always the best way to move? That's right, Sam, the Tortoise and the Hare. Pacing, or how fast you go, is very important if you want to move well. Going fast uses a lot of energy and makes us feel tired. Some of the time we want to try different speeds, so that we don't have to stop so soon to rest. If you ever play soccer you will run a long way, 5 miles, during the game. You have to change from fast to slow speeds and back to make it through the entire game. For long distances, move slowly. As you go home today, see how fast different people go—sports stars, airplane pilots, painters, sales people, and, of course, animals. Sometimes it's good to be a tortoise, sometimes it's good to be a hare."

Look For

- The child's understanding of the concepts of *fast* (sudden) and *slow* (sustained).
- The child's body control while moving at different speeds, especially medium and fast.
- The child's ability to coordinate speed with the tempo of the drum beat and to adjust speed in the airplane sequence.
- The child's ability to slow down without completely stopping.

How Can I Change This?

- Change your action words to create the relevant images of fast (charge, rapid, speedy, brisk, etc.) and slow (sluggish, waddle, careful, creep, etc.).
- Change the objects, occupations, and animals to depict variations of speed.
- Use situations in sports, games, dance, and exercise that require or show fast and slow speeds. For example, stretching for flexibility should be easy and slow, whereas dancing to rap music requires quick movements.
- Use a balloon or ball to contrast fast and slow movements.

TEACHABLE MOMENTS

Show videotapes of athletes and dancers using fast and slow speeds. Use fast-forward and slow-motion functions.

Have children walk/jog with sixth-grade partners. Together they must find the speed that both of them can walk/jog for a minimum of 12 minutes. The older child helps with pace and motivation.

Have the children bring in pictures of slow- and fast-moving objects and animals.

Teach speed vocabulary with flash cards.

HOOPS AND ME

Objectives

As a result of participating in this learning experience, children will improve their ability to

- Move over, under, alongside, through, and behind objects when in personal space and when traveling through general space (K, #6)
- Assist a partner in discovering one's relationship with an object

Suggested Grade Range

Primary (Pre-K–1)

Equipment Needed

1 hula hoop for each child, noisemaker, 3 traffic cones, 1 stand for every 2 students (Figure 7.2)

Description

The children enter the activity area and select one of the hoops scattered in general space. "Boys and girls, you have 3 minutes to experiment with the hula hoop (without stands) in your own space. No talking, but quiet giggling is OK. [Signal stop.] Leave the hoops in their spaces and come over near me [away from the hoops]. I need for everyone to sit beside Mr. Buschner, but do not touch other people or me. Please listen with your ears and look at me with your eyes. Today we will be moving. We will learn the ways your body moves with the hula hoop. We could use a ball, a jump rope, or a carpet square but today we will use the hoop. We can go over, under, alongside, through, or behind a hoop. Raise your hand if you have ever crawled under or climbed over a fence. Raise your hand if you have jumped on or off your parents' bed? When you stand or sit next to something or somebody, you are sometimes connected to that person or thing.

"When you hear the signal go back to your self-spaces, without touching, and stand inside your hoop. Now lie down inside your hoop. Now make a wide shape inside your hoop. [Signal stop.] Now, it's time to work outside the hoop. Move from inside to outside the hoop on the signal. [Stop.] Now move from outside to inside trying three different ways. [Stop.] I want you to stand behind the hoop. [Move around the space, keeping the back to the wall. The children should be adjusting their position or relationship to the object as they face the teacher.] Let's try standing to the side of the hoop—now the

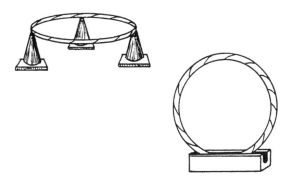

Figure 7.2 Cones supporting hula hoop; hula hoop in stand.

other side. [Signal to stop.] I wonder how smart you are. Can you stand in front of the hoop? What is happening to your body when you change your position? That's right, Nathan, you change places with the hoop. You can be alongside it, behind it, in front of it, inside it!

"Now find a way to move your body around the hoop. [Signal start and stop.] Many of you walked and ran around the hoop. This was fine. This time, find a different way, instead of walking or running, to move around the hoop. [Signal start and stop.] I want Carlos and Ashley [pinpoint, see p. 16] to show the rest of the class the special ways they moved around their hoops. There are many ways. Try to think of a way that no one has thought of before. [Start and stop.]

"We worked on moving around. Now let's move *over* the hoop. Be careful not to fall on the hoop, and always land on your feet. [Signal start and stop.] Most of you jumped over the hoop. Can you find another way to move over the hoop? [Signal start and stop.]

"Who can keep their hands inside the hoop, and move their feet around the hoop? [Start and stop.] Can you keep your feet inside the hoop, but move your arms and head outside the hoop? Let's try keeping our feet inside the hoop, but move our hands outside the hoop at a low level. [Stop.] Look at all the wonderful ways we are moving in relation to the hula hoop.

"Our next idea is to go over and under the hoop. We need to select partners—you have 10 seconds—and sit down. Partners will need three traffic cones, two hula hoops, and one stand. The idea is to make the two hula hoops stand up on top of the cones or in the stand without holding them. I want partners to work together by moving over, under, around, and through the two hula hoops. First, get ready and try moving with the hoops. Go. [Signal to stop.] I liked the way you found creative ways to move over, under, around, and through. One person will move over, under, around, and through while the other partner watches, and repeats out loud, each of the movements in relation to the hoops. [Signal to start and stop, then switch partners.]

"Boys and girls, do you remember when we worked on traveling in general space? Now, we're going to change our places with all the hoops in this large space. Everyone will move at the same time, but do not touch your neighbors. Wait for turns or find another hoop and, of course, no talking. [Signal start and stop.] I liked the way many of you were moving over, under, around, and through the hoops. I appreciated the people who set the hoops back up for others, when they accidently fell down. We will try this one more time. Try not to touch any of the hoops as you move in general space. [Signal start and stop.]

"I need the partners to gather your hoops, cones, and stands, and return them neatly beside the wall for the next class. Now, come and sit beside me one more time before we leave. What did we learn about today? No, Ethan, doing hula hoops was not our main lesson today. We used the hoop to teach us about something else. Would someone like to help out Ethan? No, Danielle, jumping was not the purpose of today's lesson. Would somebody help out Danielle? Thank you, Marta, our purpose was how we can place our bodies *with* the hula hoop or anything else. Watch Mr. Buschner [teacher demonstration]. Where is my body with this hoop [over, under, behind, beside, through, in front of, inside, outside]? Now you're getting the idea. When you play at recess, or sit at your desk, remember these place words. Let's line up *behind* Felipe. No touching, or allowing your friends to cut the line. As you walk, step *over* this hoop, walk *around* the green trash can, and go *through* the doorway. See you on Friday."

Look For

- The child's understanding of movement, as shown by their responses to your directions. Make corrections and provide helpful hints when possible, observing carefully.

- Partners cooperating and helping reciprocally.

- Safe landings when elevating the body over the hoop. Children may need to take a shorter route over the hoop to accomplish the task.

How Can I Change This?

- Use other objects for children to relate to such as balls, ropes, carpets, tables, and chairs.

- Challenge children to design an obstacle course with various equipment.

- Combine other locomotor and manipulative skills with the child's relationships to objects; for example, bounce a ball inside the hoop. Gallop around the hoop, then jump over it.

TEACHABLE MOMENTS

Design a series of task cards (large poster board with the relationship terms and drawings). These can be nonverbal cues for children to move differently in relation to the hoop.

Have partners shake hands in different ways (over, inside, outside, in front of, behind the hoop).

Have children close their eyes while moving in relationship to the hoop; partners should help with certain tasks.

Bring in pictures of athletes, dancers, gymnasts; a question might be where the catcher stands in relation to the field, pitcher, batter, plate, and umpire.

ONLY THE STRONG AND LIGHT SURVIVE

Objectives

As a result of participating in this learning experience, children will improve their ability to

- Move, using definite contrasts between heavy and light forces (1–2, #23)
- Tense and relax the muscles for heavy and light forces

Suggested Grade Range

Primary (1–2)

Organization

Large bounded area and one station for every eight students. See Figure 7.3 for stations.

Equipment Needed

Jump rope for each child; 1 chair; drum; mats and milk crates for jumping and landing; balloons, tennis balls and wall space, and Wiffle bats, tees (cones), balls for the 8 students at each station; pictures of performers

Description

The children enter the activity space, select a jump rope and begin jumping for 3 to 4 minutes (instant activity). Signal stop. "Good morning, children, today we will learn about force. Watch me as I jump from this chair 2 times and land [first heavy landing, then light landing]. What is the difference between my first and second jumps? Thank you, Matthew. The first jump had a heavy landing, making lots of force. The second one was light, and I made less force. Which would be better for my body? Correct, Mark, the light or soft landing is easier on my old bones and joints. Let's form each jump rope into a line on the ground and practice light landings each time we jump. I

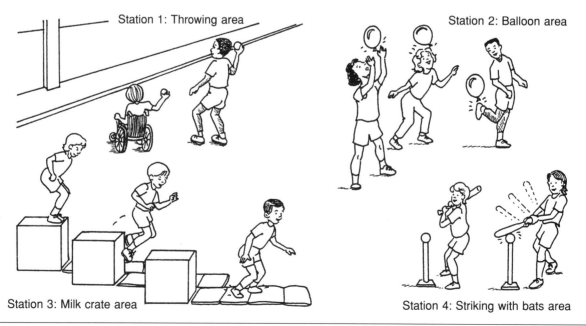

Figure 7.3 Stations for Only the Strong and Light Survive.

should not hear your feet making noise on the ground. [Signal start and stop.] This time, make a circle with your rope and sit inside the circle. Go! First we will tense up—make a muscle—in our arms. Let's count to 10. Now let go—relax those muscles. Now let's tighten the muscles in our legs, counting up to 10. Let go; relax and count to 10. Don't lie down, just feel the muscles in your legs sink down. Now scrunch up your face muscles, now let them go. OK, hit the floor with one foot using a heavy force. OK, stand up and try heavy marching in your circle, using both feet. Really stomp. Let's try a light march—walk around your circle as if it's in the clouds. [Stop.]

"When I hit the drum 1 time, I want you to move light-as-a-feather around the circle. If you hear two beats, pretend you are a strong animal on the prowl. [Start and stop.] What kind of strong and heavy animals were moving [bears, elephants, hippos, etc.]? Stand inside your circle, and pretend you are very strong, so strong that you are a weight lifter lifting a car. Show me how you would tighten and tense up your muscles to handle this great weight. You're going to press it over your head like this. [Demonstrate. Signal start and stop.] Let's go back to light forces again. This time, show me a relaxed jog in general space, slow and easy. You must save your energy and relax your arms, trunk, legs, and feet. Do not step on the ropes or circles lying on the ground. Remember how we move safely in general space without touching others or leaving the boundaries. [Signal start and stop.]

"Now that we have tried some different ways to move with light (or relaxed) forces and strong forces, I want you to practice at the stations I have organized for today. There are four stations. Station 1 is for throwing tennis balls strongly or softly against the wall. Station 2 is for tapping the balloons lightly with different body parts. Do not use strong forces at this station, because I can't afford to buy new balloons if they break. Station 3 is for light, squash landings [demonstrate] when you jump off the milk crates onto the mats. Please land on your feet; I don't want anyone to get hurt. Station 4 is for strong striking with the Wiffle bats and balls. Keep your eye on the ball before you strike, and try for a home run each time, using a strong or heavy force only—no bunts or light hitting. You will spend 5 minutes at each station, and change to a different station when you hear the drum sound. [The teacher must circulate, keeping back to the wall, and monitor the children. This is an ideal time to provide specific feedback.]

"Children, gather beside the bulletin board for the review. [There are pictures of weight lifters, gymnasts, ballet dancers, NFL linemen, golfers putting, etc.] Which of the performers use heavy and which use light forces? [Children will think that dancers' movements are light and that the football players are heavy. Guide the children to discover that all of the performers alternate heavy and light forces, depending on the situation.] Even the weight lifter probably will walk lightly, stand relaxed, and grip relaxed before any forceful movement upward. So, boys and girls, it seems we must practice tensing and relaxing our muscles for different reasons, and we must be prepared to change very fast from a light to a heavy effort, or heavy to light force. Thanks for your hard work. See you again on Tuesday."

Look For

- A clear transition between light and heavy forces; tensing and relaxing specific body parts.
- Children who are afraid to throw or strike too forcefully. They need to understand it's OK to test oneself. Similarly, some children think every movement should use great force; help them to gauge their movements, and save their energy and strength for an appropriate time and situation.

How Can I Change This?

- Use walking, running, hopping, and leaping to demonstrate both light and heavy forces.

- Provide a list and pictures of tasks to practice at each station, using heavy or light forces. The children will need additional practice time at each station.
- Try progressive relaxation exercises with children during warm-up and wind-down.
- Use manipulative equipment (foam, sock, or yarn balls) to create varying forces when throwing to a partner or target.
- Have the class practice walking down the hall quietly and stealthily (sneaky) so other children and teachers do not hear.

TEACHABLE MOMENTS

Teach the terms *force, heavy, light, easy, tense, relax, sudden,* and *sustained.*

Have the children explain and demonstrate force to their parents, friends, and family.

Have children create a force meter to determine how much force is used with particular movements.

Bring in a grip meter (hand dynamometer) to show the children how to measure strength in the hands.

MOVING SCARVES

Objectives

As a result of participating in this learning experience, children will improve their ability to

- Design a sequence with a partner in which the movements of an object are matched (3–4, #26)
- Move with a partner to music

Suggested Grade Range

Intermediate (3–4)

Organization

Large bounded area, one station for every eight children

Equipment Needed

1 scarf for each child; wands or wooden dowels, streamers, jump ropes, and hula hoops evenly distributed among the stations; drum; CD or tape player (rock, carnival, oriental music); 1 (5" × 8") index card and pencil for every 2 students; newsprint with the following list:

- Shortstop's and second baseman's matching movements in a double play
- Pair of ice skaters performing a turn and jump
- The quarterback and halfback handoff
- Guarding an opponent in basketball
- A *do-si-do* in folk dancing
- A fast break, three-on-one, in basketball
- Aerobic exercises at the Y

Description

As the children enter the gymnasium, ask each to select one scarf and practice tossing and catching it in personal space. After 4 minutes, signal to stop. "Good morning, boys and girls. Today we will be working on our relationships with objects and partners. The first task is to find different ways to move the scarves in personal space. Go! [Signal stop.] Try changing hands, catching it with different body parts, at different levels, and in various body shapes. Go! [Signal stop.] This time, drop the scarves from a high level, and try floating like the scarves to the ground. Go. [Signal stop.] Now move the scarves and your body to the music. [Music on and off.]

"Select a partner and sit down where you can see and hear me. I would like to have one person from each pair take a pencil and a card. As you hear the next music selection, I want all of you to listen to the beat and tempo, how fast the music goes. [Music on and off.] Listen once again—I'm going to lower the volume—and with your partner discuss, even draw or design, some movements to match the music. They should be movements that both of you can perform with the scarves and music. This is time to think, draw, and maybe demonstrate one piece or part, not to perform. [Music on and off.] OK, this is your chance to plan, or design and try out a movement sequence. You will practice it with your partner. Remember, the movements are to be matching and I hope you move to the music. Ready, go. [Music off.] You're doing a wonderful job. Continue practicing this sequence, so that you could teach another group if I asked you to. Make your movement sequence have a clear beginning, middle, and ending part.

"I will collect and read your cards at the end of class. Please make sure both of your names are on the cards, and that your sequences are clear. [Music on and off.] I still want you to fine-tune, or improve, your movement sequence. It may help to move side by side or together in unison. Remember, this sequence is your own creation. Let's practice it again. [Music on and off.] Now is our time to show off. I would like this half of the class to perform their routines in pairs, and this half to observe one pair. Those of you watching should look for matching sequences. [Half the class performs while half observes. Music on and off.] Now the other group will perform, and the first group will observe. [Music on and off.] Why don't we applaud all the pairs?

"The last portion of the class today involves station work and different music. You will continue working with your partner and creating matching movements to the music. You do not have to sketch your movement sequence on the cards. You can create them as you go. Station 1 has streamers; 2 has hula hoops; 3 has wands or wooden dowels; and 4 has jump ropes. You will spend 5 minutes at each station, with four pairs at each station. Then we will rotate in this direction [counterclockwise]. Ready, begin. [Each group rotates, as the teacher circulates to observe and praise the matching movements. Signal to stop.]

"Place all the equipment beside each station. Come and sit beside me or balance on your hands and one knee. Today the purpose of our lesson was—to have fun with scarves, hoops, wands, streamers, and jump ropes—not! What was the purpose of today's learning experience? Justin says that matching movements was our purpose. He's right! Who can add to Justin's answer? Thank you, Caitlin, not only matching, but performing a creative sequence of movements to music. We did use a good bunch of equipment and I hope you enjoyed the journey. What I was really watching for, though, were those matched movements. One more question before you leave. Think of examples where matched movements with a partner would be helpful to you in physical education, as you get older and better. Think for about 30 seconds. OK. Now, let's look at some examples listed on the newsprint.

"Your homework is to list 10 other situations in sports, games, dances, and exercises that involve matching sequences. They can include moving in unison and moving side by side. The list will be due the next class period, and check your spelling. You may want someone to help you with the assignment. Thanks for your hard work."

Look For

- Thoughtful and definite movement responses to matching, working in unison, and side-by-side movement.
- Opportunities to praise creative movement sequences (Figure 7.4).
- Cooperation and sharing between partners.
- Keeping to the beat of the music.
- Fluent, easy movements with the scarves and other equipment.

How Can I Change This?

- Focus on moving in a variety of pathways (circles, zigzag, and curved) during the initial activity with the scarves.
- Review sample body motions if children are having difficulty creating ideas with the scarves.
- Review the variety of body shapes made with the scarves (long, narrow, twisted, round).
- Experiment with varying speed, force, and flow working with the scarves.

Figure 7.4   Look for creative movement sequences with the scarves.

TEACHABLE MOMENTS

Have the partners show their cards and sequences to other pairs. Maybe four children could match movements.

Include illustrations with the newsprint during closure.

Have the partners discuss what it feels like to move with scarves and music.

Make notations on the index cards and the homework assignment, so that children receive feedback and gain increased understanding. Posting the cards on the gymnasium or classroom walls would help demonstrate that physical education is both a mental and physical process.

SENTENCE SCRABBLE*

Objectives

As a result of participating in this learning experience, children will improve their ability to

- Distinguish between bound and free movements as they travel
- Create and perform a bound and free movement sequence with a partner (3–4, #26)

Suggested Grade Range

Intermediate (3–4)

Organization

General space

Equipment Needed

Drum, paper and pencil for each pair of children, poster board with a list of locomotor movements and motor skills (see Figure 7.5)

Description

As the students enter the physical education area the teacher asks them "Walk like robots in general space until you hear the stop signal. [Signal stop.] Walk in general space again. [Signal stop. Repeat walking in general space with frequent stop signals.] Please sit down in a designated area. The kind of movement we've been practicing is called *bound-flow*. The movement doesn't flow smoothly—it's jerky, and has lots of stops. OK, instead of walking, let's try running and jumping in general space. Ready, go! [Students should practice running and jumping with frequent stops. Signal stops.]

"There are many locomotor movements we can use to practice bound-flow. On this poster I have spelled out several motor skills. You see the commas and periods. The comma means to hesitate, or briefly pause, in your locomotor movement. The period means to stop your locomotor movement. Together we will create a bound-flow sentence that you will practice. Let's select three words. OK, walk, run, leap. Make sure your pauses—the commas—are used properly, and your stop—the period—is clean. Practice your sentence 3 times. Ready, go! [Signal stop.]

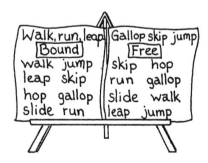

Figure 7.5   Poster board with list of locomotor movements and motor skills.

"I see you have a good understanding of bound-flow movements. Now, I want you to travel in general space as if you don't have a care in the world—like you're an eagle, soaring free in the sky. Ready, go! [Signal stop.] Can anyone tell me what was different about practicing this movement from the bound-flow movement? Yes, Joseph, you didn't have to stop. That's good, Casey. You felt you could go on forever. This type of movement is called *free-flow*. Here is the poster board with motor skill terms on it. Can anyone tell me why the comma and period are missing? Correct, Brittany, the comma means pause and the period means stop, and free-flow movements aren't supposed to pause. Let's choose three words and practice the free-flow sentence. *'Gallop skip jump'* is a good choice. Ready, go! [Signal stop.] Some of you did an excellent free-flow sentence. Most of you are having a bit of trouble with flowing from one locomotor movement to the next. Remember, there are no commas or period. There shouldn't be any break between gallop-skip, skip-jump, and jump-gallop. [Teacher demonstrates smooth transitions from one word to the next.] Practice 3 more times. Ready, go! [Signal stop.] There you go, yes, much better free-flow sentences.

"The next step to understanding bound- and free-flow is for you and your partner to make up your own sentences and practice them. Here's pencil and paper, the poster board is over there if you need some hints. Ready, go! [Have the partners practice their movement sequences, then perform for half of the class.] Great job, partners and audience. Your performances were right on! In the last activity today each of you will create and perform your own sentence, and your partner will try to guess if it's bound or free. Make two sentences each. Ready, go! [Signal stop.]

"Come sit and tell me what we learned today? Yes, Ryan, the difference between bound- and free-flow movements. And is this a free-flow movement? [Teacher demonstration.] No! I am stopping frequently; it's bound. Correct? What were the two key punctuation marks we used in the bound- and free-flow sentences to help us understand better? [Students yell, "comma" and "period."] A little more quietly, what's a comma? Right, a pause! What's a period? A stop! Can you give me any examples of bound- and free-flow movements that might occur in sports or everyday life? [Bound—walking with an object balanced on your head, boxing, driving in heavy traffic. Free—flying a hot air balloon, floor exercise routine in gymnastics, a long race.] Those are all good examples, class."

Look For

- The student's ability to correctly perform bound- and free-flow.
- The student's understanding of the differences between bound- and free-flow.
- The student's ability to work cooperatively with a partner.

How Can I Change This?

- Use other action words (explode, sneak, shrink, etc.).
- Include equipment to help demonstrate flow (scarves, wands, etc.).
- Use music to inspire creativity or enhance the experience. Rap and classical music can demonstrate contrasts between bound and free.

TEACHABLE MOMENTS

Use videotapes or pictures depicting various bound- and free-flow movements or activities.

In small groups, have the children discuss how they feel moving in both ways. "Which do you prefer?"

Chapter 8

Learning Experiences for Locomotor and Nonlocomotor Patterns

This chapter includes five learning experiences within the category of motor skills often termed *traveling* or *locomotor* skills. LEs have been developed for the subcategories of jumping and landing; skipping; running and leaping; sliding; and chasing, fleeing, and dodging. The following outline provides a glance at the focus and the suggested grade range of each LE.

Focus	Name	Suggested grade range
Jumping and landing	Knees and Ropes	Pre-K–1
Skipping	Sports Skipping	1–2
Running and leaping	Leap for Life	3–4
Sliding	Name That Movement	3–4
Chasing, fleeing, and dodging	Dodge and Freeze Tag	3–4

KNEES AND ROPES*

Objectives

As a result of participating in this learning experience, children will improve their ability to

- Take off and land while bending the knees
- Continuously jump a swinging rope (K, #13)
- Swing a rope cooperatively for a partner

Suggested Grade Range

Primary (Pre-K–1)

Organization

Small groups on large playground area

Equipment Needed

1 medium-length jump rope for every 3 students, 1 drum

Description

"Boys and girls, reach out your arms like this [demonstrate]. Stand at least an arm's length away from your neighbors, so you don't touch. I want you to jump up and down on your two feet. Ready, go! [Signal stop.] Remember, when you go into the air and land, bend your knees. Ready, go! [Signal stop.] I want you to have your knees bent a little bit to push off and land [demonstrate]. Ready, go! [Signal stop.] Some of you still have stiff legs when you land. Bend your knees a little to push off—it helps to create power to jump high. Bend your knees a little to land because that helps to cushion your landing, so you won't hurt your knees and back. Let's try it again. Ready, go! [Signal stop.] Much better jumping and landing that time.

"Each group of three children, you have a jump rope lying on the ground. I want everybody to stand on the same side of the jump rope. [Circulate among children, commenting on their positions.] Jump sideways with two feet over the rope and land on both your feet on the other side. Ready, go! [Signal stop.] Each time you hear the drum sound, jump over the rope. Show me your best jump. You do not have to all jump at the same time. Ready, go! [Signal stop.] OK, you've practiced jumping and landing in place over a rope that isn't moving.

"Now we are going to learn to turn the rope. Two partners each hold one end of the jump rope. Now swing the rope gently from side to side. [Teacher pinpoints.] Be sure to let the third partner have a turn to swing the rope. After 10 swings, trade. I'll count with you. Ready, go! [Signal stop.] The people holding the ends of the rope are called *turners*. Their job is very important. They must make the rope swing smoothly and evenly to help the jumper. With each drumbeat swing the rope smoothly from side to side. After 10 swings, trade. Ready, go! [Signal stop.] Very good, smooth swings that time.

"I think all of you are ready to put the jumping part and the swinging part together. The third person should stand between the turners and on one side of the rope. Do this now. Yes, all of you are standing correctly. Turners, with every drumbeat swing

*This learning experience was contributed by Vanessa Bryan, an elementary specialist at Durham Elementary School, Durham, California.

the rope gently from side to side, but not over your head. Jumpers, jump up and down as the rope passes under your feet. Remember to land by bending the knees. After 10 swings, we will trade. Ready, go! [Signal stop.]

"Children, lay the ropes straight on the ground and gather around me. We learned a lot about jumping and landing and swinging a rope. What's one important thing to know about jumping up? Correct, Bryan, always land on your feet. Should we jump high or low? Low. How about landing, what's important about that? Very good, Marta, we bend our knees so we will not hurt ourselves. Show me how you bend your knees one more time when you take off and land."

Look For

- Did the jumpers bend their knees on the jump and the landing?
- Can the children jump continuously, with control and keeping the knees bent (see Figure 8.1)?
- Did the children land on their feet?
- Did the children demonstrate buoyant landings?

How Can I Change This?

- For those students who are ready, swing the rope over the head of the jumper.
- Sing jump-rope songs that are familiar to children.
- Practice "Jumping Snakes" (a squiggly, grounded rope) with a partner, before using groups of three.

Figure 8.1 Look for continuous, controlled jumping with knees bent.

TEACHABLE MOMENTS

Have upper-elementary students demonstrate good jump-rope skills to the class.

Display pictures of sports figures and amateur jump-rope teams using jump-rope training/skills.

Have the children fill out smiley face surveys about their ability to jump and land.

SPORTS SKIPPING

Objectives

As a result of participating in this learning experience, children will improve their ability to

- Sequence a step-hop pattern, using both sides of the body to perform the skill of skipping (1–2, #18)
- Use skipping as a transitional locomotor pattern in combination with walking, jogging, running, galloping, and sliding

Suggested Grade Range

Primary (1–2)

Organization

Large bounded area

Equipment Needed

Hula hoop for each child, drum, CD or tape player, music

Description

As the children enter the activity area, they are encouraged to find a space and hula hoop, and practice hopping with either foot for 2 minutes. "Good morning, children. I hope you had a great weekend. Today we will work on skipping. Many of you already know how to skip, so I hope to help you get even better at this motor skill. For those of you who do not know how to skip, you will learn today. Watch Mr. Buschner skip across the ground. What are my legs doing? They are moving quickly, but see if you can find two movements. I am putting together two movements—a step and a hop. The trick to this skill is using both sides of the body, the left and right sides. Let's all stand inside our hula hoops and when you hear the signal, practice a step and hop only. [Demonstrate. Signal start and stop.] Now let's try a step and hop with the other foot. [Signal start and stop.] Next we will step and hop, but change feet and sides of the body. We will move around and outside our hoops this time. [Signal start and stop.]

"Let me have all of you with dark hair [then light, then red] place your hoops beside the wall and come right back to your self-space. When I give you the signal, try to skip in general space. Remember, this is a step and hop. [Signal start and stop.] One more time, don't touch your neighbors. Change your pathways—you can go curved, straight, or zigzag—as you skip. [Signal stop.] Terrific. Now you're ready to lead the parade at Disneyland or Disney World. All of you probably know that Mickey and Minnie Mouse lead the parade of characters by skipping. Wait for the music. [Music on and off.]

"If the skip is hard for you, we can help. Choose a partner (you have 10 seconds) and stand together. We are going to try some partner activities with skipping. One person will lead, and the other will follow. Watch the skipper in front of you and follow their movements. [Signal start and stop.] Now, when I sound the drum, the leader will switch directions; then the leader will be the follower [teacher demonstration]. Now let's skip with our partners, side by side. You may hold hands with your partner if it seems to help you. [Signal start and stop.]

"We are going to try to improve our skipping. We want to make the movement smoother and easier. See if you can relax your shoulders and your arms while you skip with your partners. [Signal start and stop.] This time, let's have partners skip to the music, no touching other partners. You may lead and follow or move side by side. [Music on and off.] OK, let's skip with partners again, but slow down when the music slows and increase your speed when the music gets faster. Stay under control and freeze when the music stops! [Music on and off.]

"Now we have our final activity. We will be changing from a run or jog to a skip, a slide to a skip, a walk to a skip, and a gallop to a skip. This will show me that you really understand how to skip. We will do this activity alone, without our partners. [Have children try each combination at least once.]

"Come sit beside me, and let's talk about skipping. By raising our hands, who remembers how we make a skip? Thank you, Karen. It is a step and a hop, using both sides of our body. Let's all spell the word skip: s–k–i–p. What is the trick to becoming a good skipper? Right on, Mark—using both sides of the body. Now, the hardest question of all, Where do we use skipping in sports, games, and dances? [Children rarely see the application.]

"Skipping is sometimes used in dancing, and often it is combined, or used, with other movements. Skipping is not used a whole lot in sports because it is much slower than running, galloping, or sliding. Basketball, football, and soccer players sometimes skip backward to guard an opponent. Skipping is like the sidestroke in swimming. How many of you know the sidestroke in swimming? Raise your hands. The sidestroke is a resting way to swim if you become tired of the front crawl or back crawl [demonstrate for the children]. You can keep moving, but you use less energy. Skipping is a fun way to rest between runs, gallops, and slides. When you want to slow down your movements, but not walk, try skipping. In fact, someday try skipping backward during recess. It takes great concentration to be a really good skipper."

Look For

- The step-hop pattern especially on the nondominant side of the body.
- Body balance and the ability to stop quickly.
- Free and relaxed arm movements.
- Opposition of arms and legs (Figure 8.2).
- Moving to the beat.

How Can I Change This?

- Have the children stay up on the balls of the feet in skipping to increase their force and speed.

Figure 8.2 Look for balanced body, free and relaxed arm movements, and the opposition of arms and legs.

- Have the children skip around cones, markers, and varied pathways.
- If the children are ready, have them practice skipping at a low level or backward.
- See if older children can combine a skip and a dribble (with either hands or feet).

TEACHABLE MOMENTS

Have the children use self-talk when skipping—encourage them to say "step-hop" while using both sides of the body.

Have groups of four children make up a movement story in which members perform a variation of skipping.

Talk about the thrill of leading the Disney parade.

LEAP FOR LIFE*

Objectives

As a result of participating in this learning experience, children will improve their ability to

- Leap, taking off and landing on the ball of the foot (3–4, #2)
- Combine a run with a leap to hurdle an object
- Rotate cooperatively among stations

Suggested Grade Range

Intermediate (3–4)

Organization

Two open playing areas for station work (set up before class) (Figure 8.3), warm-up activity, and closure

Equipment Needed

10 jump ropes; 10 hula hoops, chalk or tape to make pathways; 5 dowels, 4 small cones, 4 medium cones, 2 large cones or chairs for hurdles; extra cones to designate space; drum

Description

"Find your self-space in our open area and show me you are ready by making a statue of a frozen runner. [Wait for children to make statues.] Great, you can relax now. You

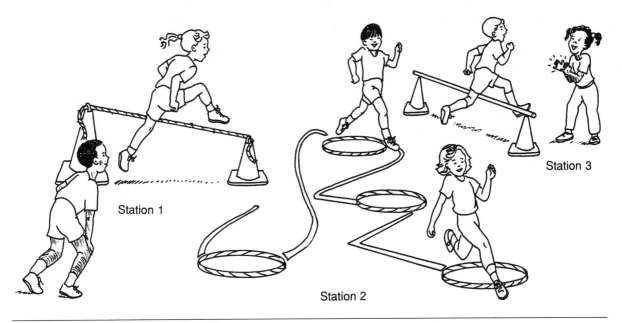

Figure 8.3   Stations for Leap for Life.

*This learning experience was contributed by Rebecca Kaiser, an elementary/adapted specialist at Colusa County Schools, Colusa, California.

have been working as a whole class on running and leaping in different ways. Today you are going to work on running and leaping together. Who can tell me some of the things that are important for running? Good—lean your body forward. Yes, move your arms opposite to your legs and push off with the balls of the feet. Everyone show me which part is the ball of the foot. Great! Now who can tell me some of the things we need to remember when we leap? Yes, really spread your legs forward and backward to get more distance. Use your arms to create momentum and land on the opposite foot. Great, you know something about how to run and leap. Let's put the two together. Warm up now by running and leaping in general space. [Start signal; stop signal.]

"Now leap, leading with the other foot. [Stop signal.] Now, each time you hear the drumbeat, leap once through the air. When you hear it 2 times, stop. [Practice; stop signal.] Great, I see that you can all run and leap keeping control and without bumping into others. Quickly find a partner and stand back-to-back. Now we will practice leaping over our friends. One person crouch down in a small ball, like a watermelon. The other partner, be very careful to leap all the way over your watermelon! On the signal your partner will practice leaping over you, taking off and landing on the ball of the foot, with a running start. When you hear the drum once, quickly change places. On two beats, stop. [Stop signal.] Any accidents? This time, run and leap over all the watermelons. Again, on one beat, those leaping will drop to the floor and become watermelons, and the watermelons will become leapers. [Switch a few times; stop signal.]

"Now we will practice running and leaping in different ways, as far as we can, as high as we can, and using different pathways. Sit down with your partner for a moment, so I can show you the different stations you will try. [Model and explain each.] With the slanted ropes, start at the small end and see if you can run and leap across to the greatest distance. With the cones and dowels, see if you can jump over the different heights. Find the one that is the most comfortable for you. Finally, run the pathways and leap over the hoops. Are there any questions? Yes, you will get to use all the stations, but don't change until you hear the signal to stop. Then I will give you directions where to go. Remember to wait your turn, if someone is in front of you, and replace the equipment for the next person if you bump it. [Send pairs to a station to practice.] You may start as soon as you get to your equipment. [Practice 5 minutes; stop signal. Repeat rotation until children have worked on each of the three stations.]

"You have done a great job of running and leaping. In a minute we will try putting the different ways together. First let's practice just running in general space where all the equipment is without bumping or touching any of it. Can you go over the equipment? No, that's right, because we are just practicing running—if we went over we would have to leap. [Stop signal.] Now let's try running *and* leaping over all the equipment. [Stop signal.] Why do you think it's important to take off and land on the ball of the foot? Yes, you then can spring up and absorb the force of landing. Now, try to find just three different pieces to leap over as you run around the general space. [Stop signal.] Run and leap over your favorite equipment. [Stop signal.] Run and leap as *high* as you can over a piece of equipment. You can use any piece. [Stop signal.] Run and leap as *far* as you can along a rope or a pathway. You did wonderfully. I saw really high leaps, long leaps, and landing on the ball of the foot. Come sit down together in our open space.

"When might you use a run and a leap together in a sport? How about in football, could you use it there? Yes—to run, leap, and catch a pass. How about in basketball? Good—to run and leap for a rebound. We also use the combination in some other sports, like running the hurdles in track. In this event you have to run as fast as you can over a whole bunch of obstacles in a row. Did anyone see this in the summer Olympics? We also use running and leaping in dance, including ballet. Let's have a PE cheer before we go. Count in Spanish this time. *Uno, dos, tres!* [Everyone shouts together] All right, PE! Get a drink if you need one, and then leap all the way back to class."

Look For

- Do the children stay on the balls of the feet for takeoff and landing?
- Can the children run and leap over successive objects at the same height? at different heights and distances?
- Are the children replacing equipment when they accidentally bump into it?

How Can I Change This?

- Try leaping in unison with a partner.
- Have one partner make a shape (i.e., wide, narrow), while the other leaps over.
- Run and leap in small groups.
- Run and leap, making a shape in the air.
- Run and leap with soft landings.
- Run and leap over a series of obstacles in a straight line.
- Combine running and leaping with catching.

TEACHABLE MOMENTS

Show a videotape of running with leaping in different sports.

Have the children run and leap, and then measure their distances. Mark takeoff and landing, measuring the distance between the two marks.

Have the children create running and leaping sequences to perform together with two or more other students.

Have the children create their own obstacle courses for running and leaping patterns.

NAME THAT MOVEMENT*

Objectives

As a result of participating in this learning experience, children will improve their ability to

- Use near and far arm and leg extensions when sliding
- Slide on the balls of the feet
- Combine sliding with pathways, relationships, and nonlocomotor movements to form a simple sequence (3–4, #8)

Suggested Grade Range

Intermediate (3–4)

Organization

Large open designated space, preferably indoors

Equipment Needed

Drum, tape player, tapes with contemporary fast and slow music, handouts (Figure 8.4) about putting together routines

Description

"Come in and find your personal space. Start stretching your body every way you can imagine—to the sides, front, back, high, low. Use every body part, including your head, neck, hands, arms, hips, back, and shoulders. [Stop signal.] Today we are going to combine many of the skills and concepts we have worked on in class. We will focus on sliding, but we are going to try it in many different ways. Later we will put our movements to music. Let's warm up with a little sliding in general space. Be sure to change directions, so that you lead with both your right and left legs. [Stop signal.] Great, you're really using the balls of your feet and bending your knees like we've practiced. This time make your arms go in and out with the rhythm of your legs to give yourself a little lift. It's like doing jumping jacks, only your arms will not go all the way up—just to the sides. [Demonstrate; start and stop signal.]"

Directions: Select at least five movements to use with your sliding routine. You may choose more.*

Relationships	Pathways	Nonlocomotor	Additional movements
Meeting/parting	Straight	Sinking	Wiggle
Leading/following	Curved	Twisting/turning	Shake
Mirroring/matching	Zigzag	Curling/bending	Float
		Stretching	Drop
			Jab

*Create some of your own.

Figure 8.4   Sample handout of movement listings.

---

*This learning experience was contributed by Rebecca Kaiser, an elementary/adapted specialist at Colusa County Schools, Colusa, California.

"I'm going to call out a pathway, and you show me how to slide in that pathway. We will change without stopping. [Start signal.] Straight! Zigzag! Curved! Zigzag! Straight! [Stop signal.] Good, I can really see the difference between your different pathways. Now I will play some fast music. [Use rap, popular, or fast baroque music that the children can relate to.] See if you can slide to the rhythm of the music. When the music stops, collapse to the floor. [Stop signal.] Great. Now I will play some slow music. As the music starts, slowly uncurl your body until you are standing. Then slide in a curved pathway. As the music gets softer, slowly stop in a twisted shape. [Stop signal.] Wonderful! I'm seeing lots of great movements. Let's move fast again. Show me fast sliding in straight pathways, with a full turn in the middle. [Change music; stop signal.]

"Now, quickly find a partner and stand face-to-face. In this position show me how to slide together around the space without bumping other pairs. You may hold hands, put your arms out, or whatever you like. Just be sure you are doing the exact same movements. Mirror each other. [Stop signal.] This time, with your partner, put a turn into your slide. You can do it at the beginning, middle, or end. Practice for a moment until you have it worked out together. [Stop signal.] With the music, now show me your sliding and turning together. [Play slow music.] Change your speed to match the music. [Play fast music.] Yes! I saw lots of variations.

"Now, try sliding together in a back-to-back position. You don't have to be touching. Again, mirror each other. [Stop signal.] We've done face-to-face and back-to-back relationships with our partners. Can you think of another way we can slide together? Yes, side-by-side. Try that now in a zigzag pathway to the music. One of you will lead, and the other follow. [Stop signal.] Switch leaders. [Play music.]

"Let's try meeting and parting. When you hear the drum, start sliding away from your partner. When you hear it again, slide back to your partner. Stop when you get back together. [Repeat.]

"We will now put several movements into a simple sequence with our partner. Start in a stretched position, face-to-face. Then use the slide with a turn that you practiced earlier and, finally, end in your stretched position again when the music stops. So it's stretch, slide, turn, slide, stretch. [Give the children a moment to figure out their movements.] OK, show me your starting positions, so I know you're ready. [Play slow music.] Now let's do it with the fast music. [Play music.] Which of you liked the fast music better? Who liked the slow music better? Great—some liked fast and some liked slow. I want you now to make up your own movements with your partner. Choose from the ones we have practiced. You need a beginning, middle, and end. Your relationship with your partner can be face-to-face, side-by-side, or back-to-back. You can move in unison or by contrasting movements. Select one of the pathways—straight, curved or zigzag. And, finally, add one or two nonlocomotor movements, like spinning, turning, twisting, and pulling. This will give you a relationship, a pathway, and a nonlocomotor movement. You have a few minutes to practice with your partner before you try them with the music. [Circulate to see how the children are doing.] All right, get in your starting positions. [Play music.] Wonderful! I saw lots of variations.

"Now that you have had a chance to practice sliding with a partner in lots of different ways, we're going to play "Name That Movement." You will make up routines in groups, and the rest of us will try to identify all of your movements. Quickly get with another pair, so your group will have four people. José and Matt, it seems we have run out of partners. Why don't you find a group of four you would like to work with, and make a group of six. When you are ready, sit down with your groups, so I can give you the directions. I will give each of your groups a piece of paper with the movements you practiced with sliding. The handout also has some additional movements you may want to include in your routines. Select at least five items to use. For example, you might start in a curled position and use meeting and parting with curved pathways as you slide apart and together. You could then put a stretch or a turn in the sliding pattern and finish in a bending position or a fall. You will also need to choose which tempo of music you would like to use from today's selection of fast or slow songs. Are there any questions? You may begin. [Allow the children 5 to 10 minutes to create their routines. Alternately play slow and fast music for the students to practice and match their movements to the tempo. Circulate throughout the room and assist groups as necessary.] Are all the groups ready? OK, I'll give you a few more minutes. [Allow groups to finish.]

"Come sit down at the edge of our general space with your group. We're ready to play "Name That Movement." Each group will have a chance to demonstrate their sliding routine to the class. The rest of us will watch and see if we can pick out what movements they have chosen. Let's be sure to give each group a big round of applause after they finish. Any volunteers to go first? Great, Latasha, your group may start. Would you like a fast or slow tempo for your routine? Get your group ready and give me the signal to start the music. [Applause when finished.] What movements did they use in the routine? Yes—sliding side-by-side, meeting, and parting. What else did you see? How about nonlocomotor movements? Yes, turning. What pathways? Yes, straight. They used one more thing that was not on the list. What was it? Right, good Sally, a kick. All right who would like to go next? How about Pepe's group? [Allow each group to perform, then analyze their movements.]

"You all created wonderful routines with sliding today. When do you think we use sliding with pathways and relationships in sports and dance? Yes—in tennis when we move back to center position. Right, in football or basketball when we follow an opponent. Do we use different pathways too? Yes, that's right: all three. How about using sliding in the polka? Has anyone seen the polka? Do we use sliding in that dance? Exactly. For homework I want you to find at least two examples of sliding that you see in real life in the next week. You might see sliding in a dance routine on MTV or in watching a sporting event. Whatever you see."

Look For

- Are the children sliding on the balls of the feet?
- Are the children able to combine sliding with pathways?
- Can the children move in unison with each other?
- Can the children make decisions cooperatively in their groups about their routines?
- Can the children get into groups independently without disputes or do they need teacher intervention?

How Can I Change This?

- Increase or decrease the number of skills they have to choose from to make a routine.
- Play "Name That Movement" competitively by giving points to teams that can guess all the movements.
- Have students bring in their own music.
- Try adding levels or additional locomotor patterns.

TEACHABLE MOMENTS

Have students match different movements to different music, depending on the tempo and rhythms.

Discuss getting into groups and how to do that efficiently and without difficulty.

Brainstorm ways to solve conflicts when people in groups want to do two different things.

Show videos of different forms of dance that use movements (i.e., modern, rap, ballet, etc.).

DODGE AND FREEZE TAG*

Objectives

As a result of participating in this learning experience, children will improve their ability to

- Use a variety of fakes
- Vary the speeds of dodging
- Dodge and tag in a game situation (3–4, #1)

Suggested Grade Range

Intermediate (3–4)

Organization

General and self-space in large bounded area (see Figure 8.5)

Equipment Needed

1 poly-spot per child, cone markers, whistle

Description:

"On the signal, walk in general space, avoiding everything you see—spots and classmates. Pretend they're poison! Ready, go! [Signal stop.] Good, I didn't see anyone touching spots or classmates. Next, I want you to vary your speed of travel. Sometimes walk fast, sometimes slow. Why is this an important skill? Sure—not to get caught and to avoid someone. Remember, no touching and no falling down. Ready, go! [Signal stop.] OK, now we will practice fakes. When you hear the signal, pretend you are going in one direction, and then quickly change and go in another direction. You might go sideways, backward, or forward. [Demonstrate.] Ready, go! [Signal stop.] Let's watch Michael, on my signal, use the three different directional fakes. [Pinpoint.] OK. This time, practice the different directional fakes without my signals. [Signal stop.]

Figure 8.5   Organizational layout for Dodge and Freeze Tag.

*This learning experience was contributed by Vanessa Bryan, an elementary specialist at Durham Elementary School, Durham, California.

"We have been practicing various dodging skills, but all of them have been in the upright and high position. Girls, dodge at a medium level; boys, dodge at a low level. At a signal you'll switch levels. Ready, go! [Signal stop.] This time you will repeat the same dodging activity, except that I will *not* give you a signal. You can choose to dodge at medium and low levels as necessary. Ready, go! [Signal stop.]

"Next we are going to practice dodging and tagging skills in an activity called "Dodge and Freeze Tag." Half of the class will stand on the poly-spots and tag people as they try to get past you. The other half of the class will try to dodge through the taggers to the opposite end, the line of safety. If you are tagged, freeze where you are. Freeze by placing your hands on top of your head until you are unfrozen [a tag by a friend] by another dodger. When you get unfrozen, continue to dodge your way through the taggers to the opposite end. Taggers, remember to touch—not push—and dodgers, use all your practiced skills. Ready, go! [Signal stop.]

"Today we practiced various dodging skills at high, medium, and low levels. We worked on backward, sideways, and forward fakes. What are some techniques you had to use to dodge successfully? Correct, Trisha: spreading out and looking for openings. Very good, Seth: keeping your balance when changing directions. Can we name at least three sports where dodging is an important skill? OK—football, basketball, and soccer. In your daily routine do you use dodging skills? You bet—riding a bike to school and walking in the crowded hallways. I would like you to think tonight about all the common dodging situations you experienced during the day. Write them down and bring the list to PE tomorrow."

Look For

- Are the students using an appropriate dodging skill for the situation?
- Did the students distinguish between the levels and the directional fakes?
- Are the students moving safely in general space without bumping or falling down?

How Can I Change This?

- Incorporate ball-dribbling skills.
- Have the students make different shapes (wide, narrow, twisted, etc.) with their body while dodging or tagging.
- Buddy up with a partner to practice the different fakes in a confined area.

TEACHABLE MOMENTS

Develop vocabulary using display posters with chasing, fleeing, and dodging terms.

Show videotapes of proficient chasing, fleeing, and dodging or videotape students practicing these activities.

Chapter 9

Learning Experiences for Manipulative Patterns

This chapter includes six learning experiences within the category of motor skills. LEs have been developed for the manipulative subcategories of catching, throwing, dribbling with hands, striking, and kicking. It should be noted that throwing and catching are typically combined and practiced when learning the majority of manipulative patterns. The following outline provides a quick glance at the focus and the suggested grade range of each LE.

Focus	Name	Suggested grade range
Catching	Egg Catching	Pre-K–1
Throwing	Carnival Throwing	Pre-K–1
Throwing	Spring Training	2–3
Dribbling with hands	Dribble Tag	3–4
Striking	Step and Swing	3–4
Kicking	Kicking Review	3–4

EGG CATCHING*

Objective

As a result of participating in this learning experience, children will improve their ability to

- Catch at a high and low level (1–2, #11)

    –For a low ball, fingers point down with little fingers together

    –For a high ball, fingers point up with thumbs together

Suggested Grade Range

Primary (Pre-K–1)

Organization

Scatter formation, self-space in large bounded area

Equipment Needed

1 playground ball for each child, drum, 1 poly-spot for each child, 4 hula hoops to contain balls at edge of general space, 2 types of stickers (1 sticker for each child)

Description

Set one ball on each poly-spot. "Find a personal space with a ball. You may begin playing with it in any way you like, as long as you stay in your personal space. [Allow a few minutes for the children to experiment with the equipment. As they are experimenting, walk around and give each child a sticker; alternate two different types, so they come out evenly. Stop signal.] Today we are going to pretend our playground balls are eggs. Show me how you could toss an egg up in the air and catch it, without letting it touch the ground. [Stop signal.] What happens if I throw the egg way out in front? Will I be able to catch it? How about if I throw it behind my head? [Demonstrate and allow the children time to solve the problem.] If I want it to drop straight down into my hands, how should I toss it? That's right, throw it straight up, just above your head, so that it will land right in your hands. [Practice; stop signal.]

"Now, show me how to catch your egg at a high level. Reach way up for it and watch it all the way as it falls into your hands. [Stop signal.] Now, show me how to catch it at a low level, all the way down by your feet. [Stop signal.] Which way is easier? This time toss your egg and catch it at your stomach. [Stop signal.] See how many different places around your body you can catch the ball. Try by your shoulder, or by your knee, by your back, or wherever you want. [Stop signal.]

"Now, let's pretend our eggs are made of rubber. Try to bounce and catch it. Drop it to the floor and catch it the first time it bounces. [Stop signal.] If the ball doesn't come all the way back up to my hands, what should I do? That's right, I can bounce it harder. Or I can reach down for my egg. Try tossing your egg really high, let it bounce one time and then catch it. [Stop signal.] You are all doing so well in your personal space. Let's try catching while we move in general space. Toss your egg up in the air as you move through general space and catch it *before* it hits the ground. Remember to look for other people; be sure not to bump them. You will have to look out of the sides of

---

*This learning experience was contributed by Rebecca Kaiser, an elementary/adapted specialist at Colusa County Schools, Colusa, California.

your eyes to watch the ball and see other people at the same time! Everyone, put your hands up in front of your eyes. [Model about 12 inches from the face.] Look at your hands. Can you still see out of the sides while you look straight ahead? This is called *peripheral* vision, or side vision. Now toss the ball and catch it in general space using your side vision so you don't bump into anyone. [Stop signal.]

"If I throw the ball straight up and walk forward will the egg drop right into my hands? [Demonstrate.] No, it might land on my head, that's right. What should I do so I can catch it? Good, throw it in front a little. Try again, tossing your egg out in front. [Stop signal.] Now, just like you bounced and caught your egg in personal space, bounce and catch it in general space. Push the egg out in front of you as you walk. [Stop signal.]

"Now you can play catch by yourself, so let's see if you can play it with a partner. When you hear the signal, find someone who has a sticker that looks like yours. Find a partner fast. [Signal.] You and your partner choose which egg you will use. [Collect extra balls.] Stand back-to-back with your partner. Hand or pass your egg over your head and between your legs, around and around. You will be moving the egg around your body with your partner. [Demonstrate; signal start and stop.] Now try to pass the egg to the side, around and around [still in a back-to-back position]. Remember to turn and look for it on the other side each time after you pass it. [Practice.] Try going in the other direction. [Practice.] Now, each time you hear a drumbeat, change directions. [Start slow and make sure everyone has their ball in control. Circulate to observe. Signal to change directions. Gradually time changes faster and faster. Stop signal.]

"Now face your partner and play catch. Remember to watch and reach for the egg. Make sure your partner is ready before you throw. [Stop signal.] Throw the egg ball to your partner so they can catch it at a *low* level. [Stop signal.] Which way should your fingers point? That's right, they point down. Are your thumbs or your pinkies together? Good—your little fingers are together. Try to throw the ball now so your partner can catch it at a high level. Really make them stretch for the egg but not too high over their head. [Stop signal.] Now which way do your fingers point, when you catch high? Yes, up. Are your thumbs or pinkies together? Right—your thumbs point together. Now try throwing the ball to different places around your partner so they really have to follow it and reach for the egg: high, low, to the side. But try to keep it close enough to them so they will be able to catch the ball.

"Now we will play a game with our partners. I call it *one-step*. Start very close to your partner and every time you catch the egg, take one step back to make it a little harder. See how far away you can get. If you drop the egg, just start again close together. [Have one pair of children demonstrate a few tosses.] Remember to catch the egg with the correct finger and hand positions. [Stop signal.]

"Skip to the closest hoop and put your ball away. Now come sit down with me in the middle of our space. Today we pretended our playground balls were eggs. Show me how I should point my fingers when I catch a ball high [children model]. How about when I catch a ball at a low level? Great! Where should I look when I am catching? Yes, at the ball. Side vision (or peripheral vision) helps you to see lots of things at once—to watch the ball and the people around you. Try to play catch with something at home. You can use a beanbag, a sock ball, or even a shoe. Let's have a PE cheer before we go back to class. One, two, three! [Everyone together shouts] All right, PE!!"

Look For

- Are the children catching with the hands only?

- Do the children move toward the ball?

- Do the children use proper hand position when catching at high and at low levels (see Figure 9.1)?

Figure 9.1   Look for proper hand position when children throw and catch balls at both low and high levels.

How Can I Change This?

- Use different types of objects (i.e., beanbags, yarn balls, paper balls, beach balls. *Note*. With some objects you may have to eliminate bouncing).
- Have the children toss and catch to music, either by themselves or with a partner.

TEACHABLE MOMENTS

Have a high-school baseball catcher come into class and talk about catching.

Have children cut out pictures from sports magazines of people catching and make a class collage out of them.

Show slides or a video of catches in different sports.

Encourage children to return stray balls to the owners politely.

Have children practice getting into pairs quickly. Have them try changing partners quickly, so they don't remain with their best friends. Reinforce working cooperatively with everyone, not just best friends.

You can have the children find someone who has the same or the opposite sticker. Try using sport stickers that depict different types of balls to match.

CARNIVAL THROWING*

Objectives

As a result of participating in this learning experience, children will improve their ability to

- Practice overhand and underhand throwing (K, #11)
- Identify body parts used in throwing
- Step with the foot opposite the throwing arm (1–2, #10)

Suggested Grade Range

Primary (Pre-K–1)

Organization

Self-space, general space, and wall space in large designated area

Equipment Needed

1 yarn ball for each student, 4 hula hoops to contain yarn balls, tambourine or drum, 1 poly-spot for each student, 60 empty soda cans in 2 or 3 bags

Description

Scatter poly-spots around the space. Yarn balls and the bags of cans are placed inside four hula hoops at the four corners of the playing space to be used later in this lesson. "When you come in the gym today I want you to skip to your own personal space. Today we are going to pretend we are at a carnival. We will practice ways to throw for the carnival. First, let's warm up our bodies and the parts that we will use [demonstrate with the children]. Show me how you touch your poly-spot with one hand, one elbow, one shoulder, one knee, one foot, your stomach, your nose. [Stop signal.] Now I'm going to call out body parts quickly without showing you. Show me where they are. [Call out different parts, changing from one to another as soon as the children have them. Mix up positions that require a high and low level, such as the nose and then the stomach. This activity will reinforce their knowing the body parts you will refer to in giving them feedback about their throws. In addition, it is good warm-up.]

"Now let's practice throwing. Look around the room. Do you see the hoops and balls of yarn in each corner? On the signal I want you to go to the *closest* hoop, get a ball, and bring it back to your space. You may play with it any way you want as long as you stay in your personal space. [Ask students to point to the closest hoop to them, to check for understanding.] What should you do if you go to a hoop and someone has just gotten the last ball? That's right, go to another hoop. This is not a race and there are plenty of balls for everyone. Now, show me how to get your equipment by hopping. [Start signal. When the children return, give them a few minutes to experiment with (get used to) the yarn balls before giving any directions. Stop signal.]

"Today we will practice overhand and underhand throwing. We will begin with underhand throwing. [Demonstrate an underhand throw to the wall several times, stepping with your opposite foot, facing the target, and pointing toward the wall when you let go of the ball.] The *opposite* foot is the foot that is on the other side of the body from the hand you throw with. [Demonstrate throwing with a same-side step.] Is my

---

*This learning experience was contributed by Rebecca Kaiser, an elementary/adapted specialist at Colusa County Schools, Colusa, California.

foot on the same side or the other, opposite side from the arm that is throwing the ball? [Demonstrate the opposite foot.] Is this the same side or the opposite side? [Demonstrate for both right- and left-handed children.] Hold the ball in the hand you throw with, and stick out your opposite foot. [Check and make corrections as needed.] On my signal, find a place at the wall and practice your underhand throwing. [Start signal. Walk around and check opposition toward the target. Give individual help as needed.] Stand as near or as far as you like from the wall, so that you can control how you throw the ball. [Stop signal.] Now try to throw an underhand ball so that it rolls to the wall, as if bowling. [Give demonstration and then positive, correctional feedback as you move around the room. Stop signal.] Now try to throw the ball underhand so that it hits the wall at a high level, as if you wanted it to go over someone's head. [Feedback; stop signal.]

"Next we will practice overhand throwing. It is like underhand throwing in many ways. We will step with the opposite foot when we let go of the ball and shift our weight from back to front. This time our hand will move above our shoulder instead of below. [Demonstrate the overhand throw several times. If you have left-handed students, model both ways.] Now practice some overhand throws to the wall. [Start signal.]

"In a moment we will play the carnival game. Sit down, so I can explain what to do. You will each have a partner. You and your partner will get three cans to set up in any way you like [two with one on top, three stacked, etc.]. One of you will be the carnival person and the other will be the contestant. The contestant gets three overhand throws and then you switch places. Try to knock over all the cans in one throw. If you knock them all down on the first throw, you still get two more throws before you switch. The carnival person's job is to set up the cans, pick up the ball, and throw it back to the contestant *underhand*. The contestant must throw the ball *overhand* to hit the cans. [Demonstrate with one of the students and caution the carnival person not to stand too close.] Are there any questions?

"When you hear the signal, I want you to quickly find a partner. [Start signal.] One of you will go and get three cans from one of the bags. When you have decided with your partner who will go, show me. The children who are to get the cans will raise their hands. [As the pairs decide, and the children who are to get the cans raise their hands, send them.] When you have all your cans, you may start your carnival game. [Check that the children throw overhand at the cans and underhand back to their partners.] Make sure you stand back far enough so it is not too easy. If you can knock them down on the first throw, try moving back. See how far back you can go and still hit the targets. [Allow the children to practice throwing and rotating. Look for opposition in arm and leg. Stop signal.]

"Finish your last turn and put your equipment back where you found it. Then come sit down in the middle of our space. [Start signal. Make sure children are putting equipment away cooperatively. If not, stop, demonstrate, and try again. When all children are sitting, review skills.] What two kinds of throws did we practice today? Good, overhand and underhand. Which foot do you step with to throw? That's right, the opposite. Can anyone demonstrate the opposite foot for me? [Have child model.] Excellent. What did you learn when you played the carnival game? Right, again, Mary. You learned that practice throwing makes you better."

Look For

- Are the children stepping with the opposite foot?
- Are the children using the same hand consistently?
- Are the children shifting their weight from the back to the front?
- Do children fetch and return equipment appropriately?
- Can the children make decisions with their partners about who will have a turn first and who will put the equipment away?

How Can I Change This?

- Try touching two of the same body parts to the poly-spot; try touching two, three, four, or more different body parts to the spot at once.
- Play appropriate music while they are practicing the carnival game.
- Try throwing different objects (beanbags, paper balls, foam balls, etc.).
- Throw at different objects (clown faces, pumpkins, turkeys, santas, etc.) that children make out of paper plates or construction paper. Throw through hula hoops, at cones, and so on.
- Those who like to compete can keep track of their scores and compete against themselves.

TEACHABLE MOMENTS

Encourage decision-making skills and cooperation by having the children decide who will get and put away equipment.

Encourage cooperation when getting and using equipment.

Encourage considerate behavior and practice getting partners. Talk about working together and how one might feel if someone turns away from being a partner. Model and practice appropriate behavior.

Teach the children to stop balls from other groups and hand them back to their owners, rather than throwing or kicking them.

Show slides or pictures of people using the different types of throwing patterns (baseball pitching, bowling, football passing, horseshoes throwing, etc.). Can the children identify the different patterns and recognize and point out the mechanics discussed in class?

SPRING TRAINING

Objectives

As a result of participating in this learning experience, children will improve their ability to

- Use arm and leg opposition when throwing overhand (1–2, #10)
- Identify body parts that help one become an efficient thrower
- Understand how throwing can be used in a variety of games and sports (1–2, #23)

Suggested Grade Range

Intermediate (2–3)

Organization

Self-space and wall space in a large bounded area (see Figure 9.2)

Equipment Needed

1 tennis ball for each child, drum, 1 poly-spot and piece of chalk for each child

Description

"Children, find a personal space [carpet, hoop, poly-spot, etc.]. Let's move some body parts in our own spaces. On the signal, show me how many different ways you can move one arm in your own space without talking or making noises. [Signal stop.] On the signal, find all the ways that arm can move [up, down, forward, backward, sideways, over, under, around, etc.]. [Signal stop.] Let's watch Zachary's and Alice's ways and look for different directions of arm movement. Now, let's move our arm at different levels—low, middle, and high—when you hear the signal. [Signal stop.] Once again, let's move one arm close to your body, then far away from your body. Don't leave your self-space, and wait for the signal. [Signal stop.] We're going to add bending and stretching this arm. Bend your arm behind you and then stretch it in front of you. [Stop.]

Figure 9.2 Organization for Spring Training.

"Now let's begin moving one leg in different directions [forward, backward, sideways, up, down, etc.]. [Signal stop.] Again, when you hear the signal, move your leg close to your body and then far away. [Stop.] Now, it will get harder. Let's move the arm and hand that works best and the leg that's hardest to kick with at the same time—on the signal. [Signal to stop.] Let's do this in a forward direction. Watch my demonstration of a throw. [Signal start and stop.]

"Finally, let's pretend we are major league baseball players. Show me how you would throw a ball a long distance. Throw at least 10 imaginary baseballs in the next minute. You have plenty of time to make 10 throws, so make them good throws. [Signal stop. Have children leave their self-space and gather around the teacher for a brief discussion.] In February and March of each year, major league baseball players go to Florida and Arizona to practice throwing, catching, batting, running, and hitting (or striking). This is called spring training. Today we will pretend we are in sunny Florida, practicing to make a major league team. The manager tells us we need lots of practice in throwing to become good. Today's practice will focus on overhand throwing. We just used the most important body parts for throwing during our warm-up. Who remembers what those parts were? Right: arms and legs. The trick to throwing is using the *whole* body, not just the arm, and always stepping with the opposite foot. Watch me demonstrate how I throw with my right hand but step with my left foot. Today, we want the manager to see a step and throw each time we practice.

"Get a tennis ball and make sure you have plenty of space to throw against the wall. Our first drill in spring training will be the overhand throw. On the signal begin throwing your ball against the wall. Remember to make good throws—this means stepping into the throw. I'll come around to watch you. You decide how far away to stand. Don't forget to catch the ball when it bounces back. [Signal stop.] This time, start close to the wall and move back one step each time you hit the wall. Again, remember you are throwing overhand and should step forward. [Signal to stop.] Finally, grab a piece of chalk from near the wall and draw a baseball glove on the wall. When you're finished, begin throwing the ball to the glove. The manager is looking for pitchers during this drill! Count the number of times you hit the glove in the next several minutes. Ready, go!

[Signal to stop and ask the children to gather around you.] "What important skill did we practice today? Right, overhand throwing. Who remembers—raise hands—what body parts work together to make a good throw? Yes, Freddy, not just arms and legs, but *opposite* arms and legs. We always want to step and throw—why? Correct, Celina, it helps us balance and not fall down. We can throw harder and farther then, and sometimes more accurately. One final question: What other kinds of sports and games use throwing? Correct, Nathan, football, soccer, dodgeball, basketball, and bowling, to name a few.

"The baseball manager would be proud of the way you practiced in spring training today. Most of you threw overhand at least 50 to 60 times. Your homework over the weekend is to get a small ball and practice another 100 times against the wall using the overhand throw. A family member or friend should watch you and verify that you completed this assignment. Have them write their name on a piece of paper saying you practiced throwing 100 or more times against the wall."

Look For

- Are the children stepping with the opposite foot when throwing with the dominant hand? (Children who have difficulty with opposition should observe the teacher's demonstrations from different angles and watch other children who are skillful.)

- Are the children working without talking and making noises?

- Does each child demonstrate simultaneous movements with the arm and leg?

- Does the entire body generate the throw, or does the arm do all the work?

How Can I Change This?

- If time permits, have the children practice making wide shapes with the body while they throw.

- Have the children who are ready throw to partners; the catchers are first stationary and then move.

- Experiment throwing with different small objects (beanbags, a sock ball, Wiffle balls, etc.).

TEACHABLE MOMENTS

Prepare some posters with the terms *throw, catch, bend, ball*, etc.; these can become part of vocabulary development.

Show photos and videotapes of proficient throwers.

Encourage children to help each other when the ball rebounds from the wall. There is a good chance tennis balls will cross paths.

Encourage the children to catch their own ball but to stop a friend's tennis ball also when appropriate.

DRIBBLE TAG*

Objectives

As a result of participating in this learning experience, children will improve their ability to

- Dribble in different directions while traveling (forward, back, left, right) (3–4, #5)
- Dribble and change speeds while traveling (slow, fast)
- Dribble keeping the ball away from an opponent

Suggested Grade Range

Intermediate (3–4)

Organization

General and self-space in large bounded area (see Figure 9.3)

Equipment Needed

1 rubber playground ball for each child, 15 cones, 8 flag belts, 4 hoops, 1 drum

Description

"Children, take a playground ball and find a space. To begin today's lesson we will review how to dribble a ball. When you push down on the ball, use enough force to return the ball to waist level [demonstrate]. If you use too much force, the ball will bounce too high; if you use too little force, the ball won't return to you. Ready, go! [Signal stop.] Another technique to help you control the bounce of the ball is to use your finger pads. Don't slap at the ball or use a flat hand. Instead, push down with your finger pads [demonstrate]. Ready, go! [Signal stop.] From watching you practice bouncing as I walked around, I think you are ready to try dribbling. Dribbling is when you keep on bouncing the ball with your hands, using finger-pad control. Dribble your ball in self-space. Ready, go! [Signal to stop.]

Figure 9.3   Organizational layout for Dribble Tag.

---

*This learning experience was contributed by Vanessa Bryan, an elementary specialist at Durham Elementary School, Durham, California.

"If you dribble too close to your toes, what will happen to the ball? Yes, the ball could hit your toes and roll away. To avoid that happening, you need to have one foot slightly in front of the other, and the feet shoulder-width apart. Try dribbling with one hand with this wide stance. Ready, go! [Signal stop.] Remember, push down with your finger pads using enough force that the ball returns to waist level. Ready, go! [Signal stop.] Finger pads and force are key techniques to dribbling a ball successfully. What was the other key dribbling technique? Yes, Bobby, foot stance. Will you please demonstrate dribbling a ball using those three techniques? Excellent. A pro-basketball scout from the Chicago Bulls is coming to watch you dribble. Show him your best dribble. Ready, go! [Signal stop.]

"Next, we can practice dribbling the ball while traveling at different speeds. Remember, this is practice and not a competitive race. You should concentrate on controlling the ball and your body. First, you will begin walking forward, and for each drumbeat go a little faster in a forward direction until you are dribbling and running. Ready, go! [Signal to stop.] This time I want you to dribble forward, changing from slow to fast speeds as you hear the drum. Don't stop, just speed up or slow down. Ready, go! [Signal stop.] Most of you are showing me good ball and body control, and that makes for a good dribbler.

"Dribbling isn't always in a forward direction; you sometimes need to go left and right. When you slide left, you should dribble the ball with your right hand, pulling the ball along. Ready, go! [Signal stop.] Now, if we slide right, which hand should you dribble with to pull the ball along? Sure, the left hand. Ready, go! [Signal stop.] Does anyone know why it is important to use the opposite hand to the direction you are going? Correct, Tonya: to protect the ball from your opponents. In this activity you are going to combine these two skills. Every time you hear the drum, change the direction of your travel to the right or left. Let's begin sliding left. Ready, go! [Signal stop.]

"You have one direction left to practice, and it will be a challenge. It's dribbling backward. Here are two clues to help you dribble backward. Look over your shoulder and pull the ball toward your body [demonstrate]. Ready, go! [Signal stop. Students will be facing the teacher in a scattered formation.] Every time I point in a direction and say the direction—left, right, forward, backward—I want you to dribble correctly in that direction. Keep your eyes focused on me and feel the ball with your finger pads. Ready, go! [Signal stop.]

"We are going to play Dribble Tag. Everything you have practiced is in this game! Every student is dribbling a ball. Taggers with flags and a ball try to tag you. Four students will be chosen as taggers. If you get tagged or you lose your ball, freeze until a friend unfreezes [tags] you. Then continue to dribble. The hoops are called Home, where you are safe up to the count of 15. Only one person per hoop! Taggers may touch as many dribblers as possible. Their job is to freeze the entire class. Remember to stay within the boundaries. Ready, go! [Signal stop. Students gather around the teacher.] Do you think it's important to practice various speeds and directions when dribbling? Yes! Why is it important? Right on, Mike, because to play basketball you need all those skills. Are there any other games or sports that need different speeds and directions [soccer, tennis, football, hockey, etc.]? You named a lot of good ones."

Look For

- Can the students change speeds and directions on your signal without losing the ball?

- Are the students looking up, not down at the ball?

- Are the students using the finger pads, versus whole-palm slapping?

- Do the students dribble the ball safely without purposely bumping into others?

- Do the children keep their weight forward when they move backward?

How Can I Change This?

- Have the children work with partners in routines to mirror, match, and follow the leader.
- Have the children use different levels while traveling in different speeds and directions.
- Make available different sizes and types of bouncing balls.

TEACHABLE MOMENTS

Show videotapes of fine performances.

Encourage better students to help less skilled students by giving them feedback and positive verbal remarks.

Emphasize the importance of varying the force.

Make sure that students develop a working vocabulary of dribbling (*finger pads*, *dribble*, *nondominant hand*, *speed dribble*, *control dribble*, *dribble tag*).

STEP AND SWING*

Objectives

As a result of participating in this learning experience, children will improve their ability to

- Use the appropriate grip to swing the bat (3–4, #7)
- Use side orientation in preparing to swing the bat
- Work cooperatively with a partner (3–4, #27)

Suggested Grade Range

Intermediate (3–4)

Organization

Self-space and wall space in a large indoor area

Equipment Needed

1 plastic or foam bat for each child, 1 Wiffle ball for every 2 children, colored tape, cassette player with familiar-sounding baseball (organ) music, enough cones to enclose the play area

Description

"Everyone will need a partner you can work well with. Find a coned area along the wall, then sit down to wait for further instructions. Ready, go! [Music plays and stops.] On the floor, in your coned area, are two pieces of blue tape side by side. A few inches in front of the blue strip you will see a piece of red tape. This tape will help you practice foot positions when you are swinging a bat. When you are standing on the blue tape lines, the foot that is closest to the red tape steps on the red. Step and swing your arms 5 times each (without a bat). Ready, go! [Music plays. Signal students to stop. Music stops.] This foot position is called side orientation to the target. It will help you strike the ball better.

"Next extend your arms out in front of you, clasping your hands. As you step to the red tape, rotate your chest so it faces the wall. This is called *coiling*. Do this 10 times each. Ready, go! [Music plays. Signal students to stop. Music stops.] Make sure when you rotate your chest to the wall that your arms remain extended and about waist high. Repeat 5 more times. Ready, go! [Music plays. Signal students to stop. Music stops.] This time you will be swinging a bat, so everyone get a plastic bat. To hold the bat properly you place the hand you don't write with at the end of the bat and the hand you do write with just above the first hand—close together, almost touching. [Demonstrate.] Partners, check each other out on the grip. [Signal to stop.] Now practice swinging the bat 10 times each. Ready, go! [Music plays. Signal students to stop. Music stops.] As you swing the bat forward, your wrist and forearms should rotate, or turn. Watch for this rotation. [Demonstrate.] Practice a few more times. Ready, go! [Music plays. Signal students to stop. Music stops.]

"Great—you're all doing so well that we can go on to swinging at a pitch. One partner is the batter, and the other is the pitcher, who stands slightly off to the side and tosses the ball underhand. It is important to make good tosses. [Teacher and student

*This learning experience was contributed by Vanessa Bryan, an elementary specialist at Durham Elementary School, Durham, California.

demonstrate.] Locate plenty of open space for you and your partner to throw and strike. After 10 hits trade places. Ready, go! [Music plays. Signal students to stop. Music stops.] It is important for the batter to watch the ball at all times. Remember these words: step and swing. Practice hitting 10 more times each. Ready, go! [Music plays. Signal students to stop. Music stops.]

"Put your equipment away and gather around me. We learned a lot about striking at a pitched ball. What two short words describe the striking skill? Right—step and swing. Can anyone tell me about other important things to remember when striking that aren't mentioned in those two words? Yes, Tami—using the proper grip. Good, Robert—rotating your wrists and forearms. This weekend I would like you to practice striking a pitched ball 100 times. Get a friend, a sister or brother, or a parent to help you. I'll ask you how you did the next time we meet."

Look For

- Are the students using side orientation?
- Can the partners work cooperatively?
- Are the students using the appropriate grip (see Figure 9.4)?

Figure 9.4   Look for appropriate grip and stance as partners work together.

How Can I Change This?

- Have the batter hit the ball to a target on the wall.
- Have the batter hit a ball for distance to an outfielder.
- Have the batter hit to place the ball in different areas.
- Have the pitcher vary the distance from the batter.

> **TEACHABLE MOMENTS**
>
> Use a videotape to show proficient batters.
> Display a poster listing striking vocabulary.

KICKING REVIEW*

Objectives

As a result of participating in this learning experience, children will improve their ability to

- Use the inside of the foot to dribble and pass
- Use the instep of the foot to kick for distance
- Use the instep of the foot to punt for distance
- Dribble using the inside and outside of the foot (3–4, #5)

Suggested Grade Range

Intermediate (3–4)

Organization

Five large stations outside in a grassy area (Figure 9.5)

Equipment Needed

1 ball for each pair of students, 5 cards with instructions for each station (see Figure 9.6): Station 1: large general area; Station 2: 4 cones, 3 goal areas, large general area; Station 3: 10 cones to designate space; Station 4: 6 hula hoops; Station 5: 12 cones (4 large to designate goals, 8 small for side lines)

Description

There are numerous learnable pieces in this lesson. Because it is a review of most aspects of kicking, assume that the majority of the children are at the transition or mature stages of kicking. Students sit down with teacher on the grass. "We have practiced many types of kicking. Today we are going to practice all the types we have learned at five different stations. Each station has a task card posted that tells you what to do. We have practiced all of these things in class, so none of this is new. Each card has a list of pointers that can help your skills at that station. At Station 1 you will practice drop-kicking with a partner; at Station 2 you will practice your placekick; Station 3 will be for dribbling, passing, and trapping; Station 4 is where you will practice place-kicking for accuracy; and at Station 5 you will play a minigame of three-on-three soccer. You have about 7 minutes at each station. When you hear the whistle, put any equipment back exactly as you found it, so it will be ready for the next group. When all the equipment is in place, I will signal to rotate to the next station. Station 1 goes to 2, 2 to 3, etc. Where do you think Station 5 will go? Yes, to 1. [Point out the location of and task cards for each station as you explain briefly what children are to do.] Find a partner quickly and sit together. When you have your partner, I will send you to a station. Read the task card and get started. [As students pair up, send them to a station to begin.]

[Circulate among the stations to give feedback, troubleshoot, and help make adjustments and vary the tasks. After students have rotated through all the stations, signal for them to come sit down together.] "I saw lots of cooperation and good practicing as

*This learning experience was contributed by Rebecca Kaiser, an elementary/adapted specialist at Colusa County Schools, Colusa, California.

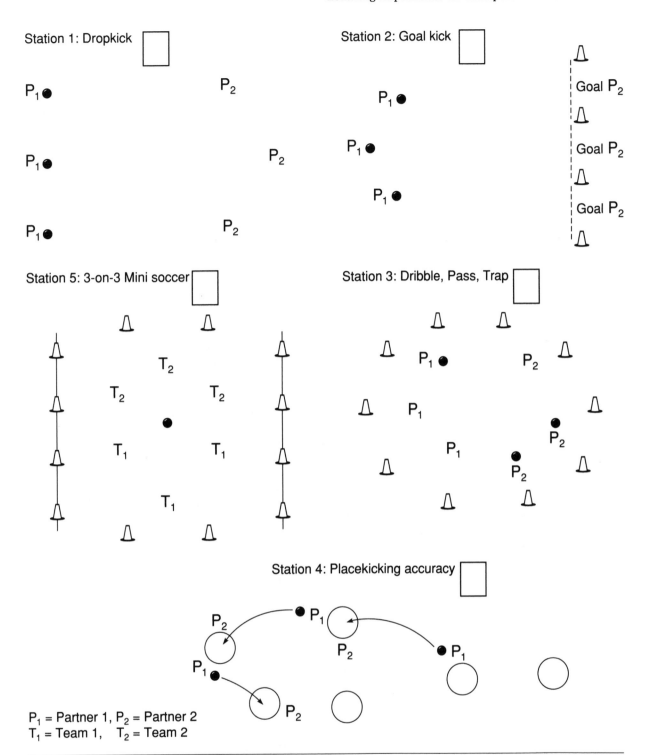

Figure 9.5 Stations for Kicking Review.

I rotated around the stations. Were any of the stations too hard or too easy? Sam, you thought that the kicking for accuracy into the hoops was hard. Yes, you're right. Why do you think this skill is important? Yes, Sue, because you have to be able to kick the ball to someone. But when do you use a placekick that you want to go to an exact spot? Good, on a corner kick and a goal kick in soccer. What do you need to remember when you placekick a ball? Yes, take two steps before you kick it. Watch the ball. Where should you contact the ball? Right, José, low and in the center with the instep of the

Task Card Station 1: Dropkick

Find an open space, away from other pairs, and practice drop-kicking to your partner. Things to remember:

1. Drop the ball to the kicking foot.

2. Look at the ball.

3. Contact the ball with the instep (shoe laces).

4. Follow through high, toward your partner.

Task Card Station 2: Goal kick

With your partner practice kicking into the goal. One person will kick 3 times, the other will stand behind the goal and retrieve the ball. Place your ball about 20 feet from the goal. Increase or decrease this distance if it is too hard or too easy. Rotate after 3 turns each. Things to remember:

1. Take two steps before you kick.

2. Contact the ball with the instep (shoe laces).

3. Follow through high, toward the target.

Task Card Station 5: 3-on-3 Mini soccer

Game play. Decide your teams by using your birthdays. First 3 birthdays in the year play against the last 3. Use the following rules in addition to any of your own.

1. Each player must touch the ball before you can score a goal.

2. If the ball goes out of bounds, it goes to the other team on the sidelines. Use a placekick or inside-of-the-foot pass to bring the ball in.

Task Card Station 3: Dribble, pass, trap

With your partner practice dribbling, passing, and trapping. Stay inside the designated space. Pass without traveling first. Then try passing around other pairs while traveling, as we practiced in class. Things to remember:

1. Dribble and pass with the inside or outside of the foot for better control.

2. Stop the ball by trapping with the bottom of your foot before passing.

3. Try to keep your head up to watch for your partner and other players.

Task Card Station 4: Placekicking accuracy

With your partner try to placekick each ball so that it travels up in the air and lands in the hoop. Try each of the different distances. Things to remember:

1. Take two steps before you kick.

2. Look at the ball.

3. Contact the ball with the instep.

4. Follow through high, toward the target.

Figure 9.6   Sample task cards.

foot. And we always follow through *how*? Great, toward the target. Before our next physical education class I want you to practice at least 50 kicks with a friend or against a wall. You can use inside-of-the-foot passes, placekicks, or dropkicks."

Look For

- Are the students stepping before they placekick or drop-kick?
- Are the students contacting the ball with the instep?
- Are the students following through high and toward the target?
- Are the students keeping their eyes on the ball and contacting it in the center and low?
- Are the students able to apply their skills in the minigame?

How Can I Change This?

- Use greater or fewer stations.
- Have more minigames.
- Kick to moving targets.
- Use balls of different sizes.

TEACHABLE MOMENTS

Watch videotapes of world-class soccer, talking about the types of kicks and the use of space on the field.

Videotape individual students and encourage them to critique their kicks.

Encourage children to work cooperatively as they go through the stations.

Have the children think of examples of kicking in sports other than soccer.

So Where Do We Go From Here?

We hope that reading this book has left you full of thoughts, some questions, and most of all, *excitement* about teaching this content area. We hope it makes you eager to get out there and try some of the ideas and learning experiences with your children . . . to take a closer look at your curriculum . . . to maybe give you that "something extra" you needed in order to take another try at teaching this content to your children.

And although we know that implementing many of the ideas in this book with your children probably won't be quite as easy as it was to read about them, we hope that this book goes a long way in helping you get there. We hope that it encourages you to talk with other teachers, ask questions, and search for solutions that will make your teaching, and your students' learning experiences, the best they can be!

We here in the Child Health Division of Human Kinetics want you to know that you're not out there alone in your quest to improve your teaching and the physical education experiences of your students. We do our best to provide you with current information and professional support through our many programs and resources.

Examples of these include our American Master Teacher Program for Children's Physical Education (AMTP), which this book is a part of; the national newsletter *Teaching Elementary Physical Education* (*TEPE*); the annual National Conference on Teaching Elementary Physical Education, which we cosponsor; and our outcomes-based student and teacher resources.

Many of you have written or called us in the past with a neat idea you wanted to share in *TEPE* with others, a question on where to find some information, or even just to say thanks for a job well done. We hope that you'll continue to let us know what your questions, concerns, and thoughts are and how we can help you even better in the future. Feel free to write us at P.O. Box 5076, Champaign, IL 61825-5076, or call us at 1-800-747-4457. We'll do our best to help you out!

Until then,

The staff of the Child Health Division of Human Kinetics

References

Allison, P. (1985). Observing for competence. *Journal of Physical Education, Recreation & Dance*, **56**(7), 50-51, 54.

Barrett, K.R. (1985). The content of an elementary school physical education program and its impact on teacher preparation. In H. Hoffman & J. Rink (Eds.), *Physical education professional preparation: Insights and foresights* (pp. 9-25). Reston, VA: American Alliance for Health, Physical Education, Recreation and Dance.

Barrett, K.R. (1988). Two views: The subject matter of children's physical education. *Journal of Physical Education, Recreation & Dance*, **59**(2), 42-46.

Barry, D. (1990). *Dave Barry turns forty*. New York: Crown.

Belka, D. (1994). *Teaching children games: Becoming a master teacher*. Champaign, IL: Human Kinetics.

Bredekamp, S. (Ed.) (1990). *Developmentally appropriate practice in early childhood programs serving children from birth through age 8* (expanded ed.). Washington, DC: National Association for the Education of Young Children.

Bressan, E., & Weiss, M. (1982). A theory of instruction for developing competence, self-confidence, and persistence in physical education. *Journal of Teaching in Physical Education*, **2**(1), 38-47.

Briggs, M.M. (1975). *Movement education: The place of movement in physical education*. Boston: Plays.

Buschner, C. (1989). Teaching for affective responses in physical education. In I. Sonnier (Ed.), *Affective education: Methods and techniques* (pp. 97-103). Englewood Cliffs, NJ: Educational Technology.

Buschner, C. (1990). Can we teach children to think and move? In W.J. Stinson (Ed.), *Moving and learning for the young child* (pp. 51-66). Reston, VA: American Alliance for Health, Physical Education, Recreation and Dance.

Buschner, C. (1992, August). *Developmentally appropriate physical education: A prescription for myopia when teaching children*. Paper presented at the National Conference on Teaching Children Physical Education, Waterville Valley, NH.

Council on Physical Education for Children. (1992). *Developmentally appropriate physical education practices for children*. Reston, VA: National Association for Sport and Physical Education.

Doyle, W. (1980). *Student mediating responses in teaching effectiveness*. Denton: North Texas State University. (ERIC Document Reproduction Service No. ED 187 698)

Elkind, D. (1988). *The hurried child: Growing up too fast too soon*. Reading, MA: Addison-Wesley.

Fitts, P., & Posner, M. (1967). *Human performance*. New York: Academic Press.

Franck, M., Graham, G., Lawson, H., Loughrey, T., Ritson, R., Sanborn, M., & Seefeldt, V. (1991). *Physical education outcomes: A project of the National Association for Sport and Physical Education*. Reston, VA: National Association for Sport and Physical Education.

Gabbard, C., LeBlanc, E., & Lowy, S. (1987). *Physical education for children*. Englewood Cliffs, NJ: Prentice Hall.

Gallahue, D. (1989). *Understanding motor development: Infants, children, adolescents* (2nd ed.). Dubuque, IA: Brown.

Gallahue, D. (1982). *Developmental movement experiences for children*. New York: Wiley.

Gentry, V. (1985). Curricular models of elementary physical education: Traditional and contemporary. *Physical Educator*, **42**(2), 59-64.

Gilliom, B. (1970). *Basic movement education for children: Rationale and teaching units*. Reading, MA: Addison-Wesley.

Graham, G. (1985). Commitment to action: Looking at the future through rear view mirrors. In H. Hoffman & J. Rink (Eds.), *Physical education professional preparation: Insights and foresights* (pp. 145-157). Reston, VA: American Alliance for Health, Physical Education, Recreation and Dance.

Graham, G. (1987). Motor skill acquisition—An essential goal of physical education programs. *Journal of Physical Education, Recreation & Dance*, **58**(7), 44-48.

Graham, G. (1992). *Teaching children physical education: Becoming a master teacher*. Champaign, IL: Human Kinetics.

Graham, G., Holt/Hale, S., & Parker, M. (1987). *Children moving: A teacher's guide to developing a successful physical education program* (2nd ed.). Mountain View, CA: Mayfield.

Graham, G., Holt/Hale, S., & Parker, M. (1993). *Children moving: A reflective approach to teaching physical education* (3rd ed.). Mountain View, CA: Mayfield.

Griffin, P.S. (1982). Second thoughts on affective evaluation. *Journal of Physical Education, Recreation & Dance*, **52**(2), 25, 86.

Haubenstricker, J., & Seefeldt, V. (1986). Acquisition of motor skills during childhood. In V. Seefeldt (Ed.), *Physical activity & well being* (pp. 41-102). Reston, VA: American Alliance for Health, Physical Education, Recreation and Dance.

Haywood, K. (1986). *Lifespan motor development*. Champaign, IL: Human Kinetics.

Hellison, D., & Templin, T. (1991). *A reflective approach to teaching physical education*. Champaign, IL: Human Kinetics.

Hensley, L., Lambert, L., Baumgartner, T., & Stillwell, J. (1987). Is evaluation worth the effort? *Journal of Physical Education, Recreation & Dance*, **58**(6), 59-62.

Higgins, S. (1991). Motor skill acquisition. *Physical Therapy*, **71**(2), 123-139.

Holt/Hale, S.A. (1993). *On the move: Lesson plans to accompany children moving* (2nd ed.). Mountain View, CA: Mayfield.

Imwold, C., Rider, R., & Johnson, D. (1982). The use of evaluation in public school physical education programs. *Journal of Teaching in Physical Education*, **2**(1), 13-18.

Jewett, A., & Bain, L. (1985). *The curriculum process in physical education*. Dubuque, IA: Brown.

Kelly, L.E. (1989). Instructional time: The overlooked factor in PE curriculum development. *Journal of Physical Education, Recreation & Dance*, **60**(6), 29-32.

Kirchner, G. (1992). *Physical education for elementary school children* (8th ed.). Dubuque, IA: Brown.

Kruger, H., & Kruger, J.M. (1982). *Movement education in physical education: A guide to teaching and planning* (2nd ed.). Dubuque, IA: Brown.

Laban, R., & Lawrence, F. (1947). *Effort*. London: Unwin Brothers.

Logsdon, B., Barrett, K., Ammons, M., Broer, M., Halverson, L., McGee, R., & Roberton, M.A. (1984). *Physical education for children: A focus on the teaching process* (2nd ed.). Philadelphia: Lea & Febiger.

Magill, R. (1989). *Motor learning: Concepts and applications* (3rd ed.). Dubuque, IA: Brown.

Masser, L. (1990). Teaching for affective learning in elementary physical education. *Journal of Physical Education, Recreation & Dance*, **62**(7), 18-19.

McGee, R. (1984). Evaluation of processes and products. In B.J. Logsdon, K. Barrett, M. Ammons, M. Broer, L. Halverson, R. McGee, & M.A. Roberton (Eds.), *Physical education for children: A focus on the teaching process*. Philadelphia: Lea & Febiger.

Melograno, V. (1979). *Designing curriculum and learning: A physical coeducation approach*. Dubuque, IA: Brown.

Nichols, B. (1986). *Moving and learning: The elementary school experience*. St. Louis: C.V. Mosby.

North, M. (1973). *Movement education: A guide for the primary and middle school teachers*. London: Maurice Temple Smith.

Paris, S., Lawton, T., Turner, J., & Roth, J. (1991). A developmental perspective on standardized testing. *Educational Researcher*, **20**(5), 12-20.

Payne, G., & Isaacs, L. (1991). *Human motor development: A lifespan approach* (2nd ed.). Mountain View, CA: Mayfield.

Placek, J. (1983). Conceptions of success in teaching: Busy, happy and good. In T.J. Templin & J.K. Olson (Eds.), *Teaching in physical education* (pp. 46-56). Champaign, IL: Human Kinetics.

Postman, N., & Weingartner, C. (1969). *Teaching as a subversive activity*. New York: Dell.

Purcell, T. (1994). *Teaching children dance: Becoming a master teacher*. Champaign, IL: Human Kinetics.

Ratliffe, T., & Ratliffe, L. (1994). *Teaching children fitness: Becoming a master teacher*. Champaign, IL: Human Kinetics.

Rink, J. (1985). *Teaching physical education for learning*. St. Louis: Times Mirror/Mosby.

Roberton, M.A., & Halverson, L. (1984). *Developing children—their changing movement: A guide for teachers*. Philadelphia: Lea & Febiger.

Romance, T. (1985). Observing for confidence. *Journal of Physical Education, Recreation & Dance*, **56**(7), 47-49.

Safrit, J. (1990). *Introduction to measurement in physical education and exercise science* (2nd ed.). St. Louis: C.V. Mosby.

Schmidt, R. (1991). *Motor learning and performance: From principles to practice*. Champaign, IL: Human Kinetics.

Schmidt, R. (1988). *Motor control and learning: A behavioral emphasis*. Champaign, IL: Human Kinetics.

Schurr, E. (1975). *Movement experiences for children* (2nd ed.). Englewood Cliffs, NJ: Prentice Hall.

Schwager, S. (1992). Relay races—Are they appropriate for elementary physical education? *Journal of Physical Education, Recreation & Dance*, **63**(6), 54-56.

Seefeldt, V. (1979). Developmental motor patterns: Implications for elementary school physical education. In C. Nadeau, W. Halliwell, K. Newell, & C. Roberts (Eds.), *Psychology of Motor Behavior and Sport* (pp. 314-323). Champaign, IL: Human Kinetics.

Siedentop, D. (1991). *Developing teaching skills in physical education* (3rd ed.). Mountain View, CA: Mayfield.

Silverman, S. (1991). Research on teaching in physical education. *Research Quarterly for Exercise and Sport*, **62**(4), 352-364.

Stanley, S. (1977). *Physical education: A movement orientation* (2nd ed.). New York: McGraw-Hill.

Stipek, D., & MacIver, D. (1989). Developmental changes in children's assessment of intellectual competence. *Child Development*, **60**, 521-538.

Thomas, J. (Ed.) (1984). *Motor development during childhood and adolescence*. Minneapolis: Burgess.

Thomas, J., Lee, A., & Thomas, K. (1988). *Physical education for children: Concepts and practices*. Champaign, IL: Human Kinetics.

Veal, M. (1988). Pupil assessment issues: A teacher educator's perspective. *Quest*, **40**, 151-161.

Werner, P. (1994). *Teaching children gymnastics: Becoming a master teacher*. Champaign, IL: Human Kinetics.

Wickstrom, R. (1977). *Fundamental motor patterns* (2nd ed.). Philadelphia: Lea & Febiger.

Williams, N. (1992). The physical education hall of shame. *Journal of Physical Education, Recreation & Dance*, **63**(6), 57-60.

Wilson, N. (1976). *The frequency and patterns of selected motor skills by third and fourth grade girls and boys in the game of kickball*. Unpublished master's project. University of Georgia.

Suggested Readings

The majority of written sources on the subject of elementary physical education espouse a traditional philosophy or the 20-fun-games-and-sports curriculum. From this perspective writers advocate, both implicitly and explicitly, multi-activity programs, typically seen at the secondary level, or the sorts of "fun activities" associated with grammar schools of yesteryear. These writers often neglect a theoretical basis for teaching the movement alphabet. The traditional model, in fact (see chapter 3), gives only superficial treatment to the movement alphabet. In one anonymous textbook (over 600 pages long) only 5% of the content concerns the movement concepts and motor skills; over 30% deals with teaching the complex sports and games. The remainder of the text allocates theory 18%, idiosyncratic programs 15%, gymnastics 18%, dance 9%, and other 5%. This type of book is familiar; the table of contents features sections on beanbag activities, parachute fun, volleyball, and numerous games and relays. Teachers should be skeptical; much of the literature disguises traditional practices with developmental terminology.

In traditional texts typically only a chapter or two directly addresses the movement alphabet: Perhaps the authors assume that curricular time should go to preparing children for secondary physical education. In short, the secondary programs and youth sports drive the elementary physical education curriculum, often to the detriment of children's developmental needs. Nevertheless, the discriminating teacher can find developmentally based books. These 15 books make a contribution to improving the child's learning of the movement alphabet.

Gabbard, C., LeBlanc, E., & Lowy, S. (1987). *Physical education for children.* Englewood Cliffs, NJ: Prentice Hall.

The authors propose six levels (instead of grades) in designing elementary physical education. Levels 1 to 3 are to provide a movement foundation, while levels 4 to 6 focus on complex sports and games. This is a helpful way to consider how children learn. Important chapters include "Locomotor Skill Themes," "Nonlocomotor Skill Themes," "Manipulative Skill Themes," and "Movement Awareness Themes" (movement concepts). Each chapter includes sections on what to observe, movement variability (often in conjunction with the movement concepts), teaching hints, and skill concepts or terms teachers can use with children. Chapter 3 ("The Scientific Basis for Motor Skill Acquisition") is short but strong; it provides a practical overview of Schmidt's schema theory linked to motor patterns with movement awareness themes. I caution teachers who attempt to implement the enhancement activities (dynamic games and relays) for levels 1 to 3 to be sure that children already have mature enough motor patterns.

Gallahue, D. (1982). *Developmental movement experiences for children.* New York: Wiley.

This book complements Gallahue's 1989 text, providing practical ideas for teachers to refine a child's fundamental and sport abilities. Eighty percent of the text is applied information about the movement alphabet, and entire chapters discuss each of the locomotor, stability (nonlocomotor), and manipulative patterns. Chapters include developmental sequence checklists, teaching tips, and activities (guided discovery, exploratory, and skill development). The photographs and illustrations help teachers analyze children's movement patterns. He includes sections on concepts children should know and six chapters on integrating application tasks and skill themes (rhythms and perceptual-motor activities).

Gallahue, D. (1989). *Understanding motor development: Infants, children, adolescents* (2nd ed.). Dubuque, IA: Brown.

This is a scholarly source for teachers who really care to understand motor development and the stages of learning motor skills from infancy through adolescence. Gallahue provides a logical presentation and a developmental framework (hourglass model). His model includes a fundamental movement phase, when most children learn the motor skills. Within this phase children's abilities can be classified as either initial, elementary, or mature. Gallahue includes a precise description of each motor skill as well as illustrations of each stage and component analysis. Chapter 11, while research-based, is a practical approach to help understand the sequence of fundamental movements (locomotor, stability movement, and manipulative). Teachers may not be able to plan lessons from only this text, but they will gain the necessary knowledge about how children acquire motor skills. The chapter on developmental physical education offers a curricular model to help teachers combine the movement concepts and motor skills.

Graham, G., Holt/Hale, S., & Parker, M. (1993). *Children moving: A reflective approach to teaching physical education* (3rd ed.). Mountain View, CA: Mayfield.

These authors have helped, more than any others, to shape the developmentally appropriate physical education movement. Their skill themes and movement concepts ideas have greatly influenced my thinking about children and content. The authors suggest considering a child's motor skills in terms of generic levels (precontrol, control, utilization, and proficiency) instead of gender, grade, and age. The approach is sound, evolving from recent research and practices. Shirley Holt/Hale directs a demonstration school for elementary physical education in Oak Ridge, TN. This book is readable, its language indicating concern with better analysis of movement. The text explains the movement alphabet (skills and concepts) and includes numerous lesson ideas, from simple to complex. This comprehensive and essential source certainly could persuade teachers to abandon old-fashioned elementary physical education.

Haywood, K. (1993). *Life span motor development* (2nd ed.). Champaign, IL: Human Kinetics.

Haywood's undergraduate motor development text provides an introduction to motor behavior over the entire life span to help readers understand and appreciate the process of developmental change. The chapters on motor behavior from childhood through adulthood detail normal developmental changes in children and youth. Haywood writes beneficial sections on the characteristics of inefficient and efficient jumpers and the developmental sequences of overarm throwing.

Hoffman, H., Young, J., & Klesius, S. (1981). *Meaningful movement for children: A developmental theme approach to physical education*. Needham Heights, MA: Allyn & Bacon.

This book provides a holistic view of physical education for children based on the premise that teachers should shift from teaching movement activities to designing conceptual learning experiences. Movement is only one part of the teaching and learning equation. The alternative organizing centers include becoming aware, becoming independent, accepting and expressing feelings and ideas, accepting responsibilities and acting cooperatively, improving quality responses (refining motor skills), and drawing relationships.

Holt/Hale, S.A. (1993). *On the move: Lesson plans to accompany children moving* (2nd ed.). Mountain View, CA: Mayfield.

This paperback includes nearly 200 pages of lesson plans for the skill themes and movement concepts in the companion text, *Children Moving* (see Graham et al., 1993). It stimulates thinking about class context, content, methods, and experience levels. Most of the lesson suggestions are rich with ideas for teaching the movement alphabet, going beyond what can be accomplished in a single class period. The set-induction ideas, task progressions, assessment questions, and practical evaluation forms are especially helpful. This is the only lesson plan book I would recommend to teachers of elementary physical education.

Human Kinetics. (in press). *Teaching for outcomes in elementary physical education: A guide for curriculum and assessment*. Human Kinetics: Champaign, IL.

This unique resource is divided into two parts. Part I introduces the concept of purposeful planning (creating curriculum goals or outcomes that are realistic and achievable for your particular situation) and then shows how to assess these goals using portfolio and performance task assessments. Teachers will find the many practical hints helpful, especially concerning the use and scoring of these assessments. Part II is organized according to the concepts (including fitness concepts) and skills taught in physical education and provides sample performance and portfolio tasks; teachers can use many of these to directly assess NASPE "Benchmarks," which are referenced when applicable. The "learnable pieces" are detailed for each skill and concept, along with activity ideas and practical hints for teaching them at the varying grade levels.

Keogh, J., & Sudgen, D. (1985). *Movement skill development*. New York: Macmillan.

In their own words, the authors attempt to provide an "overview of previous research and current thinking about movement skill development." They include some important findings from empirical research to consider in observing the motor skills and spatial-temporal accuracy of young children. Although the writing is technical, this challenging work should not be overlooked.

Kruger, H., & Kruger, J.M. (1982). *Movement education in physical education: A guide to teaching and planning* (2nd ed.). Dubuque, IA: Brown.

Providing a comprehensive analysis and interpretation of Laban's movement framework, the authors include numerous ways to teach movement themes (concepts) from a developmental perspective. Chapter 5 goes into depth about the movement concepts. Sixteen units about the movement education viewpoint conclude with application chapters on educational games, gymnastics, and dance.

Logsdon, B., Barrett, K., Ammons, M., Broer, M., Halverson, L., McGee, R., & Roberton, M.A. (1984). *Physical education for children: A focus on the teaching process* (2nd ed.). Philadelphia: Lea & Febiger.

This formidable book has become a classic source for movement educators. It emphasizes Laban's movement framework, while addressing teaching processes, principles of motion, and motor development. This source includes thought-provoking lesson themes for educational games, dance, and gymnastics.

Payne, G., & Isaacs, L. (1991). *Human motor development: A lifespan approach* (2nd ed.). Mountain View, CA: Mayfield.

This is an introductory motor development text in the same tradition as Gallahue (1989) and Haywood (1993), advancing a life span approach to acquiring motor skills. Chapter 13 ("Fundamental Movements of Childhood") gives the necessary attention to the primary motor skills. The developmental sequences (that include charts and illustrations) are particularly helpful for hopping, catching, general striking, and punting.

Roberton, M.A., & Halverson, L. (1984). *Developing children—their changing movement: A guide for teachers*. Philadelphia: Lea & Febiger.

This brief, yet informative, paperback is a well-documented guide to motor development and motor skill acquisition, from the viewpoint of potential holism in physical education for children. Although the motor skill sections use idiosyncratic terms (i.e., locomotion on feet and other body parts, sending objects away), the ideas are easily understood. Nonlocomotor skills and the movement concepts are addressed only partially, but the developmental sequences, charts, and teaching implications for the locomotor and manipulative skills are stronger.

Schurr, E. (1975). *Movement experiences for children* (2nd ed.). Englewood Cliffs, NJ: Prentice Hall.

Schurr's text is the most traditional of these sources. I selected it because the author integrates movement with sports, games, gymnastics, and dance. Her analysis of basic movement will enlighten readers about the movement concepts and motor skills. Schurr's concern that teachers must help children refine and combine the motor patterns is evident. In addition, the chapter on body mechanics is an excellent overview.

Thomas, J., Lee, A., & Thomas, K. (1988). *Physical education for children: Concepts and practices*. Champaign, IL: Human Kinetics. These authors suggest four levels of skill development—(a) becoming aware of movements and objects; (b) controlling and combining movements; (c) refining specific skills; and (d) applying specific skills—in this elementary textbook. Its developmental perspective of how children develop movement skills and learn motor skills and planning the curriculum address the subjects in a helpful way.

Wickstrom, R. (1977). *Fundamental motor patterns* (2nd ed.). Philadelphia: Lea & Febiger. Eight chapters comprise this book, an introduction and chapters on walking, running, jumping, throwing, catching, striking, and kicking. The premise is understanding each skill well enough to move children toward mature patterns. Wickstrom favors research and theory over practical ideas; however, this classic text should help teachers analyze movement patterns.

About the Author

Craig A. Buschner is a professor in the Department of Physical Education at California State University, Chico, where he teaches courses in undergraduate elementary physical education and graduate curriculum and pedagogy. He is also an instructor in the American Master Teacher Program.

In 1976, Craig received his EdD in physical education from Oklahoma State University. Since then he has trained preservice and inservice teachers in Mississippi, Texas, and California. He also has become a leader in the movement to replace traditional physical education curricula with programs that teach developmentally appropriate movement concepts and motor skills.

Craig is the discipline coordinator for physical education in the California State University Institute for Teaching and Learning. He has written numerous articles and book chapters about changing the way physical education is taught in school. Craig is a member of the American Alliance for Health, Physical Education, Recreation and Dance, the National Association for Physical Education in Higher Education, and the American Educational Research Association.

AMTP
American Master Teacher Program for Children's Physical Education

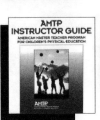

DATE DUE			
AUG 1 8 1997			
SEP 2 2 1997			
OCT 1 3 1997			
MAR 2 2 2001			
OCT 1 9			